WHAT PEOPLE SAY ABOUT ATTRACT CLIENTS

Lloyd Williams is one of the few advisors I met over nearly a decade ago as a financial advisor that I not only listened to, but modeled. He inspired me to become a fee-based advisor, when my firm wasn't even offering fee-based products. He has always been an advocate for putting the client first. His book can help you make a difference in your clients lives and your own life.

DAVID BACH
BESTSELLING AUTHOR
SMART WOMEN FINISH RICH, SMART COUPLES FINISH RICH, THE AUTOMATIC MILLIONAIRE, and *START LATE FINISH RICH*

Lloyd focuses on the crucial experience that must be sold first – the unique experience that the client has with an advisor. Once this is sold the products and services sell themselves. This is a very in-depth and practical book. A must for every advisor who wants a future that's bigger than the past.

DAN SULLIVAN
AUTHOR AND FOUNDER
THE STRATEGIC COACH. INC.
The Laws of Lifetime Growth, How the Best Get Better

The workshop is more than just about building a fee-based business. It's about taking your business to the next level using a process that clients buy into and stay with for the long-term. It's about attracting new relationships and raising new money, both of which you must manage. Concentrating on growth efficiently enables advisors to provide the services their clients value.

TONI BJORKLUND, SR. VICE PRESIDENT
PROFESSIONAL DEVELOPMENT, PIPER JAFFRAY

Lloyd Williams brings with him not only a wealth of experience but very unique insight into the ways in which advisors and their clients think.

DON HOWDEN
BRANCH MANAGER, RAYMOND JAMES

The "Client Conversation" asks the best clients, "What is truly important to you?" and then we build a solution around what is truly important for the client. As a result of the client conversation my compensation is not purely financial, but is enriched with my relationship with my best clients.

DICK BLAKELEY, CIMA
BLAKELEY GROUP, SMITH BARNEY

While the rest of the industry was trying to figure out how to transition to fee-based pricing Lloyd had already done it and was guiding us in the process.

JOSEPH M. FLAMMIO, CFP
THE FLAMMIO FINANCIAL TEAM, A. G. EDWARDS

We have found that the relationship conversation strips the conversation with the client down to what is really important to them. It puts things into perspective and gives you a better understanding not only of what the client may need financially but also emotionally. We find that we learn more than we ever imagined about our clients and they feel a closer connection to us as a result. It makes for a much better relationship if you truly want to become a trusted advisor.

JAMES R. LAUGHTON
THE LAUGHTON WEALTH ADVISORY GROUP, WACHOVIA SECURITIES

We have found the Relationship Conversation a constructive tool which allows us to understand new and existing clients' unique history and current challenges. The benefit to us and the client is clarity of purpose and alignment of goals. We find ourselves better able to design, maintain and enhance new relationships as well as existing ones.

DAVID PORTER
SANDERS WEALTH MANAGEMENT GROUP LTD.

WHAT PEOPLE SAY ABOUT LLOYD WILLIAMS

Five years ago I was frustrated and considering changing careers. Instead of finding a new career, I was led to Lloyd Williams. Not only has Lloyd helped me better than double my production over the past 5 years with a simple, easy to follow fee-based business model, he has helped me become a better advisor, husband and father. Thanks Lloyd!

JEFF BLASER, CFP, CIMA
OWNER, RETIRECARE SOLUTIONS®

Some of Commonwealth's most memorable presentations have been those offered by Lloyd Williams and the feedback I have received from my clients relative to his value-added has always been among the best at any event he's been a part of.

WAYNE BLOOM
PRINCIPAL, COMMONWEALTH FINANCIAL NETWORK

After searching far and wide, I have found Lloyd's approach to client relationships truly unique and structured for success. Lloyd's method is the way financial advisors should be doing business. It won't be long before compliance officers and sales managers mandate this business model.

BRIAN SCHRAG, CFP
VICE PRESIDENT, NORTHERN TRUST SECURITIES INC.

I have had the pleasure of attending not only workshops and seminars but also knowing Lloyd Williams personally. The energy and excitement he brings to every thing he does is infectious. You can not help leaving a conversation with Lloyd knowing this is a man of conviction and tremendous talent.

ROYCE N. NIES, CFP
FORMER PRESIDENT OF DE FREY & CO., RESEARCH MAGAZINE HALL OF FAME

We found Lloyd's guidance and inspiration to convert our practice to fee-based to be a key element in the success that we have had. We believe that without his advice we could not have completed the process as efficiently or as quickly.

PENNY OMELL, M.ED, CIM, FCSI, CIMA
THE OMELL FINANCIAL GROUP

ATTRACT CLIENTS

A Financial Advisor's Guide to Building and Running A Practice

W. LLOYD WILLIAMS

KUTSURO PRESS

CANADIAN CATALOGUING IN PUBLICATION DATA

Williams, Lloyd, 1957-
    Attract Clients: A Financial Advisor's Guide to Building and Running a Practice - 2nd Edition/ Lloyd Williams

Non-Fiction
ISBN 978-0-9780624-5-3

1. Practice Management

Second Edition

Printed in Canada

For Mom and Dad

TABLE OF CONTENTS

FOREWORD   13

INTRODUCTION   15

WHY FEES?   17
   Why Do Fee-Based Managed Money?   18
   What is Managed Money Consulting?   18
   Two Most Important Questions   20
   A New Way to Think   23
   Funding Your Lifestyle   24
   Embrace a Fee-Based State of Mind   24

ADVOCACY MARKETING   31
   The Exponential Business™   32
   Attract Clients - Stop Selling   36
   Categories of a Relationship   39
   The Ideal Client   39
   How to Recognize the Ideal Client   40
   The Relationship Train™   43
   Sphere of Influencers   44
   General Contractor vs. Subcontractor   44
   Five Transitions When Money Is in Motion 45
   Two Types of Advocates   48
   Turn Clients Into Advocates   48
   The Importance of Pen and Paper   51
   Strengthen Your Referral Muscle   53
   Building the Professional Advisory Board 56
   Executive Roundtable   60
   Advocacy Building Luncheon   61

FIRST CONVERSATION   67

Setting Up The First Conversation   68
The Normal Marketing Process   70
Every Appointment Creates The Next   70
Uncover More Business With This Simple Script   75
The Four Differences Script   79
The Movie Theater   83
Role Play   83
Little Red Wagon Script™   84
The Lost Art of Conversation   87
The Laws of Conversation   90
Important Final Step   91

PRESENTATION   **93**
Checklist for Presentation Meeting   94
ROI vs. ROR   94
The Investment Process   96
Four Stages of Consulting   97
The Presentation   97

HANDLING OBJECTIONS   **105**
Question vs. Objection   106
Sample Objections   106

EXPONENTIAL CHANGE   **121**
Ten Month Planning   122
Ten Month Planning Process™   123
Four Steps to Implement Exponential Change   124
Vision   130

ACTION PLAN   **133**
Transitioning Process   134
Two Track Focus   138
Advisor Model Day   138

MANAGING YOUR TEAM   **139**
The Necessity of Team Creativity   140
Criteria for Building a Team   144

Service: A Two-Part Job   145
Achieving Team Buy-In   146
Criteria for Team Infrastructure   148
Cost of Not Hiring   149
The Hiring Process   151
Hiring the Right Person for the Job   154
Nine Ways to Say Thank You to Your Team   155
Team Procedures   158
Cross-Training   159
Creating an Operations Manual   161
A Team On Autopilot   163
The Exponential Business Score   165
Stop The Distractions   167

COUNTERINTUITIVE   169
Important Terms   170
Counterintuitive Questions   172
Manager Selection   177

PRESENTATIONS TO MOVE MONEY NOW   179
How to Move Stagnant Money Now   180
Event vs. Economic-Driven Corrections   180
The S-Curve   181
Ten Trends for the New Millennium   182
The River   187
The Cowles Commission of 1932   188
50 / 25 / 25 Dollar-cost Averaging   188

NEXT ACTIONS   193
Ten Most Important Next Actions   194

ACKNOWLEDGEMENTS   195

BIBLIOGRAPHY   199

ABOUT LLOYD   206

FOREWORD

Lloyd Williams was one of the first in financial services to see the role managed money would play in the lives of advisors and clients alike. In 1988, he drank the kool-aid and changed from one of the best transaction based brokers to one of the first and best managed money consultants. Since then, the industry has embraced fee-based business. However, many advisors have not, possibly because it's different, but most likely because the transition, unless done by "the book", entails the hated income reduction plan. Now, after years of being a managed money consultant, consulting firms, and coaching high-end advisors, Lloyd has written "the book". If you have already converted, read this book and tighten up. If you are in process, study it to better manage the transition. If you have not started down the path, consume the book. Do what Lloyd says.

BILL GOOD
CHAIRMAN, BILL GOOD MARKETING, INC.

INTRODUCTION

Learn by Merlin

> *"The best thing for being sad," replied Merlin, beginning to puff and blow, "is to learn something. That is the only thing that never fails. You may grow old and trembling in your anatomies; you may lie awake at night listening to the disorder of your veins; you may miss your only love; you may see the world about you devastated by evil lunatics; or know your honor trampled in the sewers of baser minds. There is only one thing for it then: to learn. Learn why the world wags and what wags it. That is the only thing, which the mind can never exhaust, never alienate, never be tortured by, never fear or distrust, and never dream of regretting. Look at what a lot of things there are to learn – pure science, the only purity there is. You can learn astronomy in a lifetime, natural history in three, literature in six. And then, after you have exhausted a million lifetimes in biology and medicine and theocriticism and geography and history and economics, why, you can start to make a wheel out of the appropriate wood, or spend 50 years learning to defeat your adversary at fencing."*
>
> -TERENCE H. WHITE, THE ONCE AND FUTURE KING

WHY FEES?

The introduction of fees changed the financial services industry forever

Fees offer numerous advantages over commissions. Most important is the ability to sit alongside the client in the investment process and independently help them achieve their objectives. Fees allow your practice to present a professional image to the marketplace. Whether you intend to do fee-based business or not, you must be able to address a fee-based solution. The following presents a case for including fee-based managed money as a part of your practice.

Why Do Fee-Based Managed Money?

"If you are not the first person to have a conversation with your client about a fee-based managed money solution, you will not be given the opportunity to be the second."
                                            - LLOYD WILLIAMS

What is Managed Money Consulting?

It seems there are as many definitions for what this business is all about as there are brokers and consultants. Many people separate fee-based from managed money, claiming the former is when they manage the money themselves, inside a fee account, and the latter is when they use outside managers to manage the assets on a discretionary basis. I use a simple definition:

"Fee-based managed money is any account for which a client's risk tolerance is profiled, an asset allocation is determined, multiple managers are hired for multiple asset classes, a process to monitor and report on the account's performance is established, and an annual recurring fee is charged."

It does not matter whether you manage the money yourself or hire outside managers, whether you use mutual funds or independent money managers, whether the account is held in custody within your firm or not. If it meets the criteria detailed above, consider it a fee-based managed money account. The process established will work with any model you choose. Throughout this book, I use the terms fee-based and managed money interchangeably.

Process, Not a Product

Fee-based managed money is not a product that a client buys, it is a process a client agrees with and continues for the remainder of their lives. Too often managed money has been sold as a product by selling a particular manager or investment. When that manager's style is out of favor, or something happens and they begin to underperform, the client becomes dissatisfied with the product and wants to fire the manager and you the advisor. If you sell managed money as a product you run the risk of being directly associated with the manager.

As a financial advisor you should be consulting your clients and aiding them in achieving their goals and objectives in life. Fee-based managed money is the process to assist you in these endeavors.

A process is a series of steps or stages that a client goes through, with you, to accomplish a given objective. Whether the client's goal is retirement, college funding, estate planning, or any number of objectives, you establish a step-by-step process to guide them along the way. Some of the tools you use in the process will be optimization software, money managers, and reporting, but these are only tools and resources. Our focus will be on the process.

The Investment Consulting Group Mission Statement

"The Investment Consulting Group offers a disciplined approach to making investment decisions by providing objective information and counsel while helping our clients attain their personal and financial goals."

Two Most Important Questions

I would like to discuss what I believe are the two most important business questions that you can ask. I call these the "Finish Well Questions."

The Finish Well Questions

I was fortunate as a young man that my father took me aside at the age of fifteen and taught me the importance of asking myself the Finish Well Questions. He encouraged me to ask them every quarter, because they would yield two results: I would meet and exceed the goals I set for myself and no trend or wave of change in life or business would ever catch me unawares. I have been faithful to that request and since age 15 have repeated the process every 90 days. It contributed greatly to the success of my team and our ability to stay ahead of the curve in our business.

One of the biggest difficulties that we have in our industry is trying to realize what is coming down the road and how to prepare for it. There are continuous changes in technology and in the demographics of our client base. New products, processes, and investment vehicles pop up every day. Today there are many choices to make that did not exist just a few years ago. These changes lead to tremendous confusion and inability for us to focus on what is most important. That lack of focus causes us, in many cases, to miss tremendous opportunities that are set before us.

To take advantage of the trends that are happening around us, I believe you need to take time once each quarter to focus. Prior to your business or quarterly planning session with your team, get away by yourself and think about the answers to the two questions. The results and new focus you gain, as well as your ability to concentrate on that which is most important, will amaze you. You will also be better equipped to direct and guide your team.

Schedule a half day. Go somewhere quiet where you will be undisturbed by phones or personal contact, to the mountains, the beach, or just go to the library - any place where you can find solitude.

Question #1

Ask yourself: What will my industry look like in three years? By asking yourself this question, you are forced to think about all of the things that surround you. You know where the industry is going and what trends are happening around you, but one rarely takes the time to actually concentrate on them. Typically a trend comes about and you are left looking back saying, "I knew that was coming," but you weren't able to act on it until it was too late.

You can reverse that pattern by taking some time each quarter to think about what will happen over the next three years. What will change in your clients's lives? What investment vehicles will rise to prominence? What new technology will exist that you can take advantage of and use to better benefit your clients or to streamline the business? How will your clients change? What new markets will surface and what new sources of assets will be out there? What will your team look like in three years? Each of these questions will help answer the broader question: Where is the industry going and what will it look like? You should take at least an hour and concentrate on your vision of the future.

Most people never take the time to ask themselves this question and then, when a trend or event affects their life, they feel overwhelmed. If they had taken time to ask the question, they would have realized they had already foreseen what was coming. They could have known that the company was looking at downsizing or relocating employees because the market they were in was no longer as productive as it had been. They could have seen that new technology would dramatically impact the way they deliver services to their clients so they could have re-tooled themselves with the new technology.

We know the facts and see them coming, but what can we do? Often we don't concentrate on the future because we think it is inessential right now; it doesn't have immediate impact on us. We forget about it and leave it alone. We do not realize that, during the time the change is developing, we could prepare our team and ourselves for the transformation.

Question #2

The first question answers what will happen. The second question helps us realize what our response or action should be.

Ask yourself: What can I do today to prepare for the future? You have to see what you need to do and how you will respond in order to prepare your team and yourself for a coming trend. Without knowing the answer to the question, knowing what the trends are does no good - it is just information. Knowing what you need to do and outlining the steps that you need to take gives you an action plan for the future. Preparation allows you to take advantage of the opportunities.

Armed with answers to the two questions, you not only know what will happen but know what your response should be. Spend about an hour on the first question and another hour on the second question. Use that time to formulate strategy. You can prepare while the trends develop. You can prepare your team, clients, technology and yourself for the change. Instead of being overwhelmed by the wave, ride the wave and benefit from its advance.

A New Way to Think

Logical Mind	Active Mind
Reason	Intuition Experience Emotion Feelings
Answers NO to every question	**Answers YES to every question**

If you live your life controlled by your Logical Mind, it will not allow input from your Active Mind. By letting the Active Mind dominate, the Logical Mind is allowed input into every decision, rewarding you with a richer perspective.

Funding Your Lifestyle

How much will it take to fund your lifestyle?	Yours	Example
Lifestyle you desire		$200,000
Payout at your production		40%
Divide lifestyle by payout for gross revenue needed		$500,000
Fee paid on fee-based business		1.00%
Divide gross revenue needed by fee paid		$50,000,000
These are the assets you need to place in fee business to fund your lifestyle.		

Embrace a Fee-Based State of Mind

There are many reasons why brokers do not switch to managed money. Over the years, I've heard a number of valid excuses, the following among them:

"I will lose control."
"The manager might steal my account."
"I will not make as much money."
"There is poor performance in the portfolios I see, and it's not very exciting."
"I will lose contact with my client."
"I am an old dog and I do not want to learn new tricks."

But when you ask consultants who have succeeded with fees about their reasons for doing managed money, you hear, "There is more control, not less, as I become the center of influence in the life of the client."

With a fee-based business you are the general contractor and the money managers become subcontractors. You are recognized as the expert and you have the time to focus on your skill of raising assets.

As you contemplate your practice today, consider the following questions: Are you able to concentrate your time and energy on what you do best? Are you spending your days involved in your best moneymaking activities, like making presentations to high net worth clients? Or are your days filled with a lot of distractions that take away from your ability to make money? If so, your business won't grow, and you won't be as successful a fee-based advisor as you might like. You can change that as you go through the process of transitioning to fees.

The Four Tasks

Making the transition from a transactional, commissioned-based business to a more fee-oriented, managed-based business can be substantially easier if you realize that managed money is not a product, but a process. It is not something sold; it is a process clients buy into and stay with the remainder of their lives.

Realize the only way you will get paid in this industry is by raising new money. Yes, you along with everyone else must find, raise, manage, and service money. Of these four tasks, only raising money really pays you.

Think about it. You are not paid to find money. If you found a $10 million account this afternoon, nothing would be paid to you until you actually closed the assets. You are not paid to manage the money because if the stock you select goes up 300% your commission does not go up 300% when you sell it. You are not paid to service money. When that lost dividend check is recovered, it does not show up as additional revenue in your account. The only way you are paid is by raising new money and growing your client base. If you have a $50 million book of business on January 1st and 12 months later you still have a $50 million client base, your revenue will not be any greater than the previous year.

The only way to increase your revenue consistently is by raising more assets. Certainly, you could increase the turnover ratio within your portfolios, but that would have to stop before the SEC or the compliance department stepped in. The fastest, easiest, and safest way to grow your business is by raising more assets.

You need to concentrate on growth. Not only do we want to transition you from a transactional, commissioned-based business to a more fee-oriented, managed-based business, but also grow your practice. Growth is an issue of change, a matter of changing your mindset from what it is now to what it could be.

Reasons Brokers Don't Do Managed Money

- Loss of control
- Fear of not being the expert
- Manager may steal account
- Not make as much
- Poor performance, not exciting
- Lose contact with client
- Don't understand, old dog/new tricks

Reasons Consultants Do Managed Money

- More control
- Recognized as expert
- Higher client retention
- More time to raise money
- More time for self and family
- Better performance with less risk
- Better information

Benefiting From Fees

The paradigm shift begins with the realization that fees are more professional. Clients recognize that salespeople deal in commission for the sale of a product. Professionals deal in fees for the delivery of a service. In moving to fees, you must change your mindset from selling to consulting. We grew up in an industry that shifted from being attraction-based in the turn of the last century to being solicitation-based today. We have to move back to an attraction-based model based on advocacy marketing and away from solicitation.

In changing your mindset, you will discover how liberating managing assets can be. In a transaction-based business your freedom is limited and you are much more closely tied to the business at hand. The quote machine becomes a daily part of your life. However, as you move to a fee-based business, freedom, independence, and the ability to have choices increase as you shift your focus from day-to-day activities to long-term planning. You will also find that your client retention rate is higher. You will have more time to raise assets and more time for yourself and your family.

Your clients will benefit as their properly allocated portfolio will experience better performance over time with substantially less risk. You will also find, as you work with your money managers, you will have access to better information. You will truly become a better expert. In that regard, I encourage you to pursue your designation as a Certified Investment Management Analyst (CIMA). If you have not looked into it, go to the Investment Management Consultant's Association (IMCA) website at www.imca.org for further information on becoming a certified consultant.

Charting a New Course

By applying the Finish Well Questions to your life and practice, you can chart a new course today. It is possible to see three years into the future, but not five or ten years out. The headlights do not shine bright that far down the road. If you get too close, the headlights shine too bright so a six-month to one-year time horizon is too short. However, you can expect about an 85% accuracy rate in predicting three years out. Look ahead three years and envision what you want your life to look like.

What is the picture of the industry and your business in particular? What can you do today to prepare? What can you do today that will groom you for the changes you see down the road?

When asked what made him such an exceptional hockey player, Wayne Gretzky said he went where the puck was going, not where it was. The Finish Well Questions should alert you to changes you foresee in your client base and industry. They should help you progress your practice and put you ahead of the game.

It is my contention that you can convert your entire

book to fees if you believe as passionately in fee-based consulting as you did in the last stock you recommended to clients. Really, your conversion to fees is an issue of what is going on in your head rather than what your clients will think. Once you become convinced of the necessity of making the transition to fees, you will have overcome your largest obstacle and be well on your way to growing your business and finishing well.

ADVOCACY MARKETING

Attraction, Not Selling, is the Key to Marketing Success

The aim of marketing is to make selling superfluous; to know and understand the customer so well that the product and service fits him and sells itself.

-PETER F. DRUCKER – THE ESSENTIAL DRUCKER

The Exponential Business™

Every business undergoes stages of change. I believe there are five stages that a business experiences to create The Exponential Business™.

What is The Exponential Business™?

The Exponential Business™ is a business that creates advantages, in both your personal and professional lives, that far outweight the effort and energy that go into realizing those advantages.

Most businesses identify the product they want to build and then try to identify clients willing to buy that product. That is the solicitation model and it has worked for many years. I believe, however, a better model is based on attraction. As Peter Drucker said, "Businesses are made up of two primary functions; the first function being marketing, and a second function being innovation." These two functions, I believe, are central to the process every business must go through.

Stage I: The Exponential Team™ – Infrastructure Development

Before you can focus on marketing you must have a team that supports your vision and compliments your skills. This stage is often overlooked and further progress is limited. Without a team infrastructure to stop distractions, control the inflow of information, fill the gaps in your personal skill set, and leverage your time and effort, you will spend years trying to accomplish what can otherwise be accomplished in months. The best investment you can make in yourself is a team to support your vision.

Stage II: The Exponential Conversation™ Marketing

For any change to happen the fundamental infrastructure of the company must properly align. The infrastructure is supported by the eight inches between the entrepreneur's ears. That is where the understanding begins as to what the focus of the business should be.

As Drucker said, "The aim of marketing is to make selling superfluous; to know and understand the customer so well that the product and service fits him and sells itself." The transformation starts by placing our focus on the client and the relationship that develops. The focus is not on our products and services, and our having to push it on the client, rather we focus on the client's needs and create a solution so our products and services draw them to us. There is a substantial difference in someone being sold something and someone buying something.

In marketing, after the entrepreneur embraces the mind-set change, it is a matter of reaching out to the team surrounding the entrepreneur and ensuring they understand the change as well, that they buy into that vision. Then, as a team, you align your procedures and tasks with that vision. The Exponential Conversation™ is a tool for building trust in your top client relationships and identifying their unmet needs.

The necessity of understanding a client's unmet need is at the heart of developing an attractive practice. If we identify the unmet need of a large group of our clients then develop that niche and provide real solutions, clients will be drawn to us.

Stage III: The Exponential Solution™ – Brand Creation

By identifying the client's primary unmet need, you are able to innovate the solution that can meet their need and build a brand around the solution. It is here that true value is added in the life of the client as you create the innovative solution to fulfill, meet and exceed their needs and expectations. The solution requires taking time to asses what you currently have to offer, what competitors offer, then creating something new and branding that solution.

The Exponential Solution™ allows you to identify the steps necessary to create your brand. By identifying a unique brand in the marketplace, you trademark your solution and processes. You establish a unique position in the marketplace relative to your peers who do not have a brand or who offer generic solutions to everyday problems. Once your brand is created, you progress to the delivery of that brand into the marketplace.

Stage IV, The Exponential Experience™ - Operational Management and Brand Delivery

The brand created, you then identify the process by which you will deliver the brand into the marketplace. You must identify the procedures necessary to deliver your solution, your brand, into the marketplace consistently, repetitively, without flaw. You must provide the "red carpet treatment" of deliveries.

The Brand is the Intellectual Property the client applies to his problem. The Experience is the Emotional Response to his time with you. The client remembers the emotional response much more than the intellectual property. It's how you said it versus what you said.

You receive referrals because of The Experience, not because of the solution. A client doesn't tell his friend what you did for him, rather how you did it.

Stage V: The Exponential Entrepreneur™ – Financial Independence

It is in Stage IV that the business accelerates and starts to run on autopilot. At this point the business begins to become fun. Most businesses never experience the autopilot state. They spend all the time trying to maintain the Operational Management Stage. They remain in Stage IV because they never master getting the business under control and the business controls them more than they control it.

However, once you have the Operational Management under control, you can focus on the profitability of the business. You can look at multiple streams of income as you see multiple brands become possible. Multiple opportunities present themselves both inside the business and other areas as your exponential results surface from your original practice and the alternate practices.

Now that the business runs on autopilot you are able, as the entrepreneur, to focus on recreating energy in yourself and in your team. Without refilling the pitcher with water, you cannot keep pouring it out. You and your organization need to reinvest in yourselves. You have been creating value in the lives of your clients. It is in the fifth stage, when the business is a perpetual money-making machine, that you have the capability to enjoy the growth you achieved and the ability to enhance your life and the lives of those around you. You begin to focus on the dreams you have, the physical, mental, spiritual, emotional, and relational sides of your life and your legacy. As these elements become more important you are able to give back at an exponential rate to what and who you care about.

Take a look at the five stages of The Exponential Business™ and identify the stage in which your business currently falls. All businesses that are successful and growing move through the five stages. Over and over, as you build different brands, you will move through these stages.

Attract Clients - Stop Selling

With the deregulation of commissions, advisors aggressively solicited clients and the reputation of the financial services profession plunged. Attracting clients is the core principal of a fee-based practice.

When I entered the industry in 1984 a financial services publication ran a list of the 100 most respected occupations. Physicians ranked first as the most respected while used car salesmen came last. Lawyers ranked second, accountants placed third, and stockbrokers ranked fourth.

In 1995, 11 years later, I reviewed the survey again. The numbers were radically different. Physicians were still in the top spot and used car salesmen were still at the bottom, however, ranking just above used car salesmen were lawyers at 99. and stockbrokers at 98. How low we had fallen in little over a decade! I wondered why that happened until I realized something dramatically changed with both brokering and lawyering from the 1970s through the '80s and '90s.

Prior to the 1970s, the various bar associations worldwide

prohibited lawyers from soliciting or advertising. Subsequently, a lawyer began to advertise. If you were hurt or injured in an accident you should call his firm, which specialized in what was then called "personal injury law" and the lawyer would get you what you deserved. The American Bar Association threatened to disbar the lawyer and his law firm and the case was taken to court. In the end the Court of Appeals ruled the lawyer had the right to advertise. This decision opened the floodgates and for the first time in the history of the legal profession we saw a blizzard of advertisements for law firms.

What happened next was a sea of change in public opinion. A firm that advertised was no longer seen as a professional, quality firm, but one that might be characterized by derogatory terms like "ambulance chasers". That perception spilled over the rest of the industry.

In the beginning, legal services sought to attract clients, not solicit them. Clients sought and retained attorneys because of their professionalism and education. A lawyer could simply hang out his shingle and clients would come. Then along came that major change in the system, the right to solicit and advertise, and in just over 10 years lawyers dropped from the second most respected profession to the second least respected.

Financial Services

The same held true for the financial services industry. At the turn of the century an individual entered this industry because of who he was and who he knew. He was usually born into a wealthy family. He had an influential father with a lot of contacts. He was educated at the finest universities and his friends were wealthy as well. In those days a broker was called "the customer's man". Clients called in asking to buy 100 shares of the new stock or buy 100 of those new railroad bonds. The client was serviced, not solicited.

The model changed radically after the deregulation of commissions. Firms then needed to attract a higher volume of sales to counter the lower commissions. They opened the doors and employed anyone who had the ability to sell. As the industry moved from attracting clients to soliciting clients, the reputation of the financial services profession plunged from fourth most respected to third least respected.

The movement from an attraction-based to a solicitation-based model is one of the primary reasons why transitioning to fees is so important in your practice today. As you switch to a consultative, fee-based practice, you also shift to a more professional, attraction-based model.

Think about the top surgeon in your community, the top tax attorney, accountant, or expert whose name comes to mind when a particular profession is mentioned at a cocktail party. That is what I mean by attraction. These professionals do not solicit business. They do not have to advertise, run direct mail campaigns, or cold call. Instead, they enjoy a constant stream of clients who want to work with them. As a matter of fact, it is only salespeople who allow clients to make the decision about who will work with who. In truly attractive professional practices the professional decides whom they want to work with and whom they do not.

Adopting a more professional model may necessitate changes in your practice. First, you need to build the infrastructure that will attract wealthy clients. You must have systems, procedures, and processes in place that facilitate their needs. Second, you need the expertise necessary to attract them: continued education, certification, and professional designations may be important. Third, you must have a team that can support the needs of high-net-worth clients. Finally, you must have a service strategy, a methodology of servicing and retaining clients, that separates you from the herd.

You cannot have a $100,000 client base and attract million-dollar clients. You cannot have a $100,000 infrastructure and attract million-dollar clients. You must have a million-dollar infrastructure to attract million-dollar clients.

Set aside some time to think about your target clients and how you could develop the team, infrastructure, strategy, and expertise that will attract your ideal clients and draw them in. Both you and your clients will benefit from your increased professionalism.

Categories of a Relationship

Advocate
Client
Customer
Prospect
Lead

Highest

Lowest

The Ideal Client

- Has Money Now
- Has Recurring Money
- Is Busy at Work or Play
- Is a Delegator

How to Recognize the Ideal Client

Use this four-point test to find clients who will appreciate your managed money expertise and refer you to their equally ideal friends.

Some of the largest stumbling blocks to happiness you will encounter in your practice is dealing with a customer who does not appreciate you, who does not use you to the fullest extent, or who does not trust you. Working with this person can turn your joy to drudgery.

Clearly such clients are less than ideal. Identifying who the ideal client is from the start can make all the difference.

The client hierarchy

In managed money relationships, people in your database fall under five categories. The first category is lead. A lead is nothing more than a name, an address, or a phone number. At this stage, it is unknown whether or not the person is qualified to work with you or is someone you would want to do business with. A lead does not have much value until you gather more information and determine if the name should move up the relationship chain.

Prospect is the second category. Once you have spoken to your lead, gathered initial information, and determined that she is someone you want to work with, she can then be categorized as a potential client.

The third category comes into play when the person actually does business with you for the first time and becomes a customer. In the brokerage industry, most relationships are really customer relationships rather than client relationships. A customer is someone who does a little bit of business with you and a little bit of business with somebody else. Gas stations do not have clients, they have customers who stop there because of the location at the time they need gas. Dry cleaners, on the other hand, have clients because a person will continue to work with the same dry cleaner as long as they continue to starch his shirts correctly. In the financial industry a customer is one who will only hold a portion of their assets with you.

The transition to the fourth category happens when the customer entrusts you with all of their assets and works with you exclusively. At this point you develop a client relationship. Client relationships are most prevalent with financial planners and investment consultants.

The most valuable relationship category, however, is the fifth, that of advocate. An advocate is a client who is willing to speak on your behalf. I believe there are two types of advocates.

Referral sources

Clients who, on a regular basis, refer you to their family, friends, or associates, and support and encourage your efforts.

References

Clients who do not feel comfortable actively referring you to someone else, but who willingly act as a reference and will explain to a stranger what it is like to work with you and your team.

Recognizing the Ideal Client

As you consider the five categories, lead, prospect, customer, client, and advocate, you must create your definition of the "ideal client". As a professional with an attractive fee-based business, you should be able to determine whom you want to work with and within what parameters.

Consider the following four criteria, an ideal client will be someone who:

Has money now
This client is not waiting for money to come. She isn't looking to win the lottery. She has money now and meets a minimum account size you predetermined.

Has recurring income
A client with a lump sum distribution will tend to start living off her assets the year after she receives her windfall. This means that each year you will have to raise more assets just to cover the declining asset base. You want clients who have recurring assets, either in new stock options or more growth in their business. You want clients who not only have enough money up front, but a pool of money that is regularly replenished.

Is busy
You want clients who are either busy working or, if retired, busy playing. A client who is retired and not busy can present constant challenge. She is the one who will watch CNBC all morning and then call you at 9:30 a.m. to ask whether or not you agree with what was said. You want a client who has a life, so you can be left to do what you do best, which is manage their financials.

Delegates by nature
Given a choice of doing something herself or delegating

it to someone else, the ideal client will always choose to delegate. A good example of someone who does not like to delegate is a hobbyist investor; a transaction-oriented client basically uses you for information, but does the bulk of her business elsewhere.

Instead, you want a client who is willing to delegate the responsibility of managing her assets to you as the consultant. It is best to ask her up front, " Are you a hobbyist investor or do you prefer to delegate that responsibility?"

Think about the clients in your database who do not meet all four criteria. In the majority of cases you will see that these clients are among your biggest problems. To make your practice more attractive to high net worth individuals, you should raise the bar on the type of clients you accept and work exclusively with "ideal clients" that meet the criteria you established. You will find that you become substantially more attractive when you are less accessible to the general public. Even more importantly, you will find yourself working with clients who not only appreciate your managed money expertise, but will promote your value to other potentially ideal prospects.

The Relationship Train™

Relationship building can be illustrated by a train with an engine, a fuel car, and a caboose. If the caboose of a train is the resulting Relationship then the fuel car is the Trust necessary to create the relationship and the engine that drives the relationship building process is Expertise. Relationships are not built by rapport building; they begin when a prospect recognizes an expert who has the knowledge to solve their problem, and they begin to determine whether they trust the individual or not.

Sphere of Influencers

Every client is surrounded by influencers: bankers, brokers, doctors, lawyers, accountants, and other professionals. Clients are encircled by these professionals and must listen to advice, assess the merit of the advice, and make decisions based on analysis. Often the client is the least qualified person to make the decision. For this reason, many clients bring into the Sphere of Influencers someone to stand beside them and be a clearing house for all of their advisors. This "Chief Advisor" has the ear of the client. You want to be that chief advisor in the life of your client.

General Contractor vs. Subcontractor

Are you practicing as a general contractor or as a subcontractor? When a home is built many subcontractors are hired, but there is only one general contractor. When a sub does a poor job painting the kitchen they are replaced because dozens of good subs are available. It is important to note that the general contractor is not fired; they do the firing. The reason being there are only a few great general contractors. Are you a subcontractor in the life of your clients or are you their general contractor?

Five Transitions When Money Is in Motion

The most important time to come into a client's life is when his or her money is in motion. Too often we are introduced to prospects with static money. They are happy with their current advisor and have no pressing need to make a change. Our job, then, necessitates finding a reason for the client to make a move.

The substantially more powerful way to build a practice is to design your business around the five times in a person's life when money goes into motion. These transitional periods offer unique opportunities because you can showcase not only the resources of your team but the resources of your outside professional advisors as well.

Each of the transition periods has several things in common. They are periods of major transition in a person's life. They are also, more importantly to you, times when money goes into motion and is available for reallocation, redeployment, and repositioning. It is a time when decisions need real insight and rational analysis to help the client better understand the situation, but also a time of emotional stress which requires patience and understanding to help the client cope.

Retirement

The first transition period, the one we deal with most in our career, is retirement. When a client retires from work and moves on to a new stage in life, most or all of their assets are available for redeployment. Group retirement plan assets, individual retirement plan money, and taxable money all come to bear. Sometimes a move is involved from a large home to something smaller. This is a time when analysis is necessary to determine income streams and make certain that wills and trusts are suitably designed. Retirement is the most prevalent transition in our industry on which we focus most of our attention, but it is not necessarily the most lucrative.

Job Change

The second major transition in a client's life is job change. When we look at corporate America, we see a game of musical chairs in the executive suites as companies pursue growth and innovation. Senior executives are hired and fired on a regular basis and, as they are, the vesting of their retirement assets and other transitional assets go into motion. Those who focus on corporate senior executives as clients may find that the same position leads to three or four new clients over the years. Each of these clients has need for stock option analysis, retirement and estate analysis, as well as a need for someone to evaluate options on salary and contract negotiation as they enter a new job situation. All these are services that you, your team, or your outside professional advisors can bring to bear.

Divorce

The third period is that of divorce. Divorce is often a devastating time. Whether the dissolution of marriage is mediated or effected through the legal process, there is a property settlement and distribution of properties. IRA assets that were once tied exclusively to the ownership of one spouse are split. Retirement assets that would have been stagnant or tied up for a number of years are released and may be passed from one spouse to another to distribute the wealth. Real estate, in many cases, must be sold, liquidated into asset value and distributed. For advisors who focus on this marketplace, this is time to be of value in the analysis, assessment, evaluation, and implementation of the strategies necessary once the divorce is final.

Resource: The Institute for Divorce Financial Analyst (IDFA) is a national organization dedicated to the certification, education, and promotion of the use of financial professionals in the divorce arena. Learn more at www.institutedfa.com.

Relocation of Elderly Parent

The fourth transitional period is the relocation of an elderly parent from his or her house. This process can be traumatic and normally involves a significant asset, like a home or land, which needs to be liquidated so proceeds can assist in the support and care of the elderly parent.

Assisting a family through this difficult time, offering comfort and understanding, strengthens the connection to the family. It also allows a stagnant asset to become an active asset for the family's use.

Death

The last transitional period is that of death, a period when hand holding is necessary and a client needs to feel comforted. Risk profiles need updating to make certain the surviving spouse does not have a lower or more conservative risk profile due to the death of their significant other. This is the one time when almost all the assets go into motion and are available for re-titling. Legal work is required to re-title the assets and redistribute them into individual accounts.

Applying The Five Transitions

The five transition periods are important because money is in motion and there is a need for value-added consulting analysis. Teams that focus their practice around these five periods, or one, two, or three of them, create niche marketplaces in their communities. They become known as the team with the expertise to deal with a transition proficiently and compassionately. Whatever the cause of the transition period, each requires significant analysis and trust is an important factor. When your team truly focuses on this market, you utilize your consulting tools and benefit from the reallocation of assets to the proper allocation going forward.

Examine your practice and current markets. Create your new niches and new markets around the five transitional periods. Instead of creating a reason for an asset move, the event itself creates the necessity for reallocation analysis and redeployment. You, as the expert, guide the way and implement the new strategies.

Two Types of Advocates

Advocates come in two types: reference and referral. Webster's definition of an advocate is, "one who speaks on behalf of another."

Turn Clients Into Advocates

Develop a business relationship with an investor and you gain a client. Develop a friendship with a client and you gain an advocate that leads to more clients, more business, and more friends.

The most desired method of marketing for new clients is always referrals. Because of the strength of endorsement from the referring party, consultants, as marketers, benefit by the ease with which a referral typically closes, as well as the trust placed in us early in the relationship. It is such a powerful marketing method that, over the years, we in the industry solicited referrals and endorsements from our friends, clients, and associates by asking directly, "Who do you know?" or "Do you know someone to whom we could be of service?"

The problem with referral marketing is that it places the client under pressure. Research indicates that a person put on the spot for information suddenly feels as if the attention of an entire room is upon him. His heart rate and blood pressure increase and his mind goes into vapor lock. Suddenly, he is stressed and tends to reply with the standard answer, "I can't think of anyone," which is the truth. Brain activity comes to a screeching halt and he literally cannot think of anyone at that moment.

This is not the way to deal with clients. This is not an emotional deposit into a client's life; it is closer to an emotional withdrawal. Stop soliciting referrals from your clients. Stop asking them directly, "Who do you know?" Instead, use what I call advocacy-based marketing.

Implied endorsements

Here's how advocacy-based marketing works. Imagine you are at a cocktail party and across the room you see your friend John talking to a person you have not met. You walk over, shake hands, and begin a conversation. At that point John turns toward the woman and says, "I would like to introduce you to my friend, Sally." You exchange smiles, handshakes, and a few words. The interaction is called an introduction.

Introductions typically happen in public spaces. Even if John does not like you, he will still smile, shake your hand, and make the introduction to Sally. Now, after you walk away, John might turn to her and say, "Stay away from that person," but the introduction still occurred. If it hadn't, John would have committed a social faux pas. What is important is that, in the midst of the introduction, even though there is no direct endorsement of you by John, Sally does infer an endorsement. You receive the benefit of a referral, but without John feeling pressured.

The lesson? Stop asking for referrals and start setting up situations that allow for introductions to be made on your behalf. The heart and soul of advocacy-based marketing is to compel others to speak on your behalf, to become advocates for you.

What is an advocate?

Like an attorney who speaks on your behalf before the court, an advocate is one who speaks on your behalf among his or her friends and associates. Think of one of your clients, perhaps an older man or woman who thinks the world of you. This individual is an advocate. She refers everyone she meets to you when the opportunity rises. Your relationship is more than just business, it's a personal relationship.

Now imagine what would happen to your business if your top 25 clients appreciated you even half as much as the advocate we just described. Your business would explode with productivity. The objective in advocacy-based marketing is not to bring in 100 new clients but, more important and more productive, to duplicate your top 25 clients. You want your top 25 clients to introduce you to one new person just like themselves. This cloning process of recreating your top 25 clients could increase your assets by 50% or more per year.

Building advocacy

How do you build advocacy among your client base? That is an imperative question.

Advocacy is not built by doing big things right. Instead, advocacy is built by doing small things right. Every firm in the industry does all of the big things the same. The trade execution at your firm is no faster or slower than at other firms and a statement in your firm is no better or worse or more readable than another firm's statement. The little things separate you from the competition. The small things you and your team do for clients set you apart.

The Importance of Pen and Paper

One of the small things that will set you apart from all other advisors is sending your top clients a personal hand written letter on fine paper, written with a fine fountain pen.

I encourage you to purchase a fine writing pen and writing paper. Write a handwritten note to one of your top 20 clients about travel, a fine restaurant, or any topic aside from business, the economy, or the market. Focus on things you would talk about as a friend and not as a businessperson. Take this time to change your relationship. Your client has likely never received something like this from any other financial service professional.

The secret to building advocacy is understanding that advocates do not view their relationship as strictly business. The way to create an advocate is to change the relationship from business to personal. Do with an advocate what you would do with a friend. Don't just play golf or go to lunch, invite him or her to dinner or to your home. Treat them as more than just a business client.

Advocacy-Based Marketing is important because it creates strong, close relationships. Even more important, as your top clients introduce you to other people just like them, your time, effort, and energy are leveraged significantly. That is where real value is created.

To get started, I encourage you to write the handwritten letters referred to above. Commit to writing one letter a week to one of your top 25 clients. If you stick with it, over the course of a year, you will have written two personal letters to each of your top 25 clients. I recommend Amalfi paper, one of the finest papers made in the world, to write a personal note and take your first step toward building fine friendships that accomplish much more than your usual business relationships.

Again, the topics to write about are non-business subjects such as travel and food. Wealthy couples enjoy travel and a good restaurant recommendation.

Resources:
Colorado Pen Company - www.coloradopen.com
Cavallini & Co. - www.cavallini.com/amalfi.html
Ashford - www.ashford.com
B. Collins Pens - 800-404-7367
Pen World Magazine

Strengthen Your Referral Muscle

Looking back at the best referral sources of my career, I realized most were individuals which my team and I created as referral sources rather than ones who naturally, through their own style and capability, made referrals or endorsements.

If you think about your own client base, you will find that a small number, often less than 1%, of your clients introduce you to a new person year in and year out. These are your Referral Advocates. The reason there are so few is that most people are not network or sales oriented. They do not live by referrals in their own business and, therefore, do not offer them themselves.

Clients typically feel uncomfortable introducing their friends and associates to you. They are uneasy about making this introduction when the relationship between you and their friend or associate may or may not work out. Because of this, when we ask for referrals we get the answer, "I can't think of anyone right now, but if I do I'll be more than happy to mention you." Of course, we all know they rarely think of anyone.

As stated before, Referral Advocates make up a small fraction of your clients. I believe there are two types of advocates to have in your client base. In addition to your referral sources, who introduce you to their friends and associates, you also have Reference Advocates. A Reference Advocate is very different from a Referral Advocate. A Reference Advocate is someone who does not feel comfortable introducing you to their associates or friends, but has no problem speaking to a stranger and answering questions about what it is like to work with you.

In my practice, we selected a number of clients whom we wanted as advocates and then asked each if they would mind acting as a reference for my team. In other words, would they be willing to answer a few questions from one of our prospects, someone they do not know, about what it is like to work with us? This approach served as a springboard for turning the client into a Referral Advocate.

Creating New Referral Sources

Once you select the list of clients you want as advocates, first and foremost, you must have a conversation with each. The conversation strengthens your relationship with the client and builds a deeper level of trust.

Next, ask if they will serve as a Reference Advocate, which solves two problems. First, your prospect gets to hear that you are capable of providing the service you say you do. Secondly, it allows your reference source, with little commitment and no risk of a broken relationship because they are dealing with a stranger, an opportunity to practice and learn the language of endorsement. They are able to practice talking about you and get comfortable talking about you and your services. The long-term benefit is that the more comfortable they become with communicating this endorsement to strangers, the easier it is to discuss this with people they know.

Learning the language of endorsement is much like presenting a new product to market. The first time you give the presentation, it may not be very good and you might stumble through it. The second time you get better. By the third time you give the presentation, you have the presentation down pat. Basically, you memorized and present the information over and over again to each client with virtually the same script. As a matter of fact, if I asked you to repeat one of your scripts from years past, you probably have it burned into your memory and can still recite it.

By repeating a presentation, you learn the language and get comfortable with it. By repeating the process of introducing you and talking about you to strangers, your reference source learns the language of endorsement. They derive their own script about you and become comfortable with it. Soon, they find they are more comfortable in talking to associates and friends about you as well.

Of the people who consistently gave my team introductions throughout my career, we realized the majority were people who started out as Reference Advocates grew into Referral Advocates with time and practice. I encourage you to apply this step-by-step process. First, profile your existing client to build a deeper, trusting relationship. Second, ask the client if they would be willing to act as a reference and talk to strangers about what it is like to work with you. Give them the opportunity to participate in such referral conversations several times. Then continue to let them know you want to grow your business with people just like them and that you would like the opportunity to be introduced to their friends and associates.

If you will try, I think you will find that this very simple process can dramatically increase your referrals. Just like you work out in a gym to build up muscle, this language of endorsement, the Referral Muscle, strengthens over time. It takes practice, and being a Reference Advocate allows the client to practice in a safe environment until they are comfortable enough to talk with their friends and associates about you.

Building the Professional Advisory Board

A client calls with a tax related question. You think you know the answer, but ask your client to give you a moment while you call one of your Professional Advisory Board members. While the client holds on one line, speed dial one of your tax professionals, who, because of your ongoing relationship, takes your call immediately. Relay the client's concern and the tax advisor not only gives you the information requested, but offers additional questions to ask the client and the reasons for those quesitons. You thank him, pass on the client's name for his reference and return to your client on the other line. After explaining the answer to the client and posing the additional questions, you determine there may be a "red flag" waving and suggest the client make an appointment to speak directly to the Professional Advisory Board member. Tell him you will make the introduction and give him the advisor's name, address, and phone number. After the call, fax the advisor a note with the client's name, address, and phone number and ask him to contact the client in three days if he has not heard from the client in the interim. Then send a confirmation letter to the client with the advisor's information. Later in the week a Professional Advisory Board member calls with a referral who needs investment management consulting help.

The value added in this situation is immeasurable. The client receives the information he needs, a Professional Advisory board member has a potential client, you enrich your service as a consultant to your client, and you reap the benefits of your professionalism.

What is a Professional Advisory Board?

A Professional Advisory Board consists of a group of professional advisors that extend and enhance the services you provide to clients. The group is established with your clients's best interests in mind. Many times the professionals a client works with on a regular basis do not take time to examine the client's whole situation. After you conduct your client profile, risk analysis, and asset allocation analysis, you have a better understanding of the client's overall situation than any of his other professionals. At the front lines, you are best able to identify potential "red flags".

How to Identify Members

Start first with your current professional advisors who already have relationships with your clients. They are always looking for new business. Simply ask your clients who their advisors are and whether they are satisfied with their services or not. If they are satisfied, explain that you are always looking for professionals to refer business and do they mind if you contact their advisor. If they are dissatisfied, you have an opportunity to introduce your client to a professional with whom you have a relationship.

If you identify a professional you want to work with, invite him to breakfast. Take the opportunity to describe the type of clients you work with and why they work with you. Tell him exactly what you do and how that is substantially different from other broker's and financial advisor's services. Then ask him to explain the services he provides that will benefit your clients.

Breakfast Meeting Agenda

- You would like to hear about the types of services their firm offers, but before you begin, tell them a little about the type of clients you work with and why they are your clients.
- Have a Relationship Conversation.
- Let him explain how his firm's services will best serve your clients.
- Try to send him a referral next week, if you like what you see.

How They Function

Every member of the Professional Advisory Board agrees to meet with all referrals you send them for a one-hour consultation to determine problems and services needed. All resulting work is billed at their normal rate. As a formalized group, you can easily structure seminars and workshops for your clients or prospective clients. What is most important is your role as the hub of the client's financial needs.

Areas of Outside Professional Advice

Wills / Trusts
You will discover that most clients have not spent adequate time exploring their estate planning needs. Ask every client when their will was last reviewed and to identify the residual trustee for their family trust. Most clients have a need for someone to review or redesign their estate plan.

Insurance Analysis
You should have every client's insurance policies reviewed

by an insurance professional. Examine the quality of the carrier, the features of the product, and the price.

Accounting and Tax Advice

Your client may be dissatisfied with their current tax advisor; use this opportunity to introduce your Professional Advisory Board to your client.

Business Planning and Development

With so many managers being "downsized", clients are faced with even broader needs. In my practice, we suggested that our clients look at consulting as a new career in their remaining pre-retirement years. Consulting allows them to gradually leave the workplace and take advantage of the many retirement planning options available to them as self-employed consultants.

Your Professional Advisory Board

Identify several professionals you can work with to extend your advisory services. The benefits of a Professional Advisory Board far outweigh the time invested. This is truly a value-added service for your existing and prospective clients.

Always Fax a Referral Notice

How many times have you referred a client that never contacted the professional? Always send a fax referral notice to inform the professional that you are making the referral. The fax creates a record of the referral that can be filed by the professional advisor's name for future reference. The sample referral notice below can be used as a simple one page fax. An e-mail could also be used, but a fax sometimes stands out more than an e-mail.

Facsimile Cover Sheet

To: Professional Advisor's Name
Company: Advisor's Company Name
Phone: (999) 999-9999
Fax: (999) 999-9999

From: Lloyd Williams
Company: Investment Consulting Group
Phone: (999) 999-9999
Fax: (999) 999-9999
Date: May 1, 2006

Pages including this cover page: 1

Comments:

The following client(s) have/has been referred to you on [Date]:

Client Name
Address
Phone

If you haven't heard from [Client Name] in 3 days, please contact them.

Executive Roundtable

After establishing your Professional Advisory Board, you can leverage this group into the corporate executive arena by conducting Executive Roundtables within the executive suites of major corporations. I found corporate executives met all the criteria for ideal clients and enjoyed the monthly educational talks.

Advocacy Building Luncheon

Advocacy-Based Marketing is based upon the concept of turning a business relationship into a personal relationship. It is a necessity in improving relationships with each of your top clients. The use of an advocacy-building luncheon can enhance your practice as well as identify those clients who are true advocates.

While referral is the most prevalent method used to promote business in our industry, the practice places tremendous pressure on the person to whom you are asking for the referral. For this reason, I urge you to stop asking for referrals and start setting up situations that allow your top clients to make introductions on your behalf instead. An introduction does not necessarily include an endorsement, but does result in the equivalent benefit from your standpoint, which is an introduction to a peer of a top client.

In order to identify Reference Advocates, I recommend advocacy luncheons.

Step 1:

Identify 10 clients within your top 25 to 30 from whom you do not receive referrals, but whom you would like to have as advocates. These are clients you would like to duplicate. Eliminate problem clients, hobbyists, or do-it-yourselfers from the list.

Step 2:

Call the first client on the list and state the following: "Mr. Jones, I have some decisions to make about my business, and I would appreciate your advice. I would like to buy you lunch next week and talk to you about it." The highest praise you can give a person is to ask for his or her opinion. No one will tell you "no" when approached in this manner. An appointment is then set for lunch.

Step 3:

During this luncheon, you have two objectives, the first is to pass along the vision you have for the future of your business and the second is to start the process of building an advocacy relationship. Begin by saying that part of your vision is to grow your practice with other clients just like him or her. "I want a practice that serves high net worth individuals and allows me to focus my time on the top clients like yourself. I have a strong support team in place to work with the existing client base and I want to focus my time and attention exclusively on the top tier clients."

Step 4:

Next, make it clear that, although this is your goal, you realize there are probably some gaps and this is the reason you seek the client's help. Perhaps you have not met or exceeded the expectations of all your top clients and you would like the advice of the person across the table to help you understand where you fall short. Write down everything the client offers.

Step 5a:

If the client says, "Everything you are doing is just fine. I am perfectly happy," you have done a good job and you can skip down to Step 9.

Step 5b:

If, however, the client has a list of items, listen carefully. You cannot hire a consultant to give you this kind of information. The client is telling you exactly what is necessary to turn him or her into an advocate. Write it down line by line. Then respond to the client by saying, "I would like your permission to touch base with you within the next 90 days to go over the new procedures and new resources we will put in place to eliminate this problem going forward. Can I have your permission to contact you then? ("Yes.") This information is extremely valuable. Thank you."

Step 6:

As soon as you get back to the office, write a thank you note and reiterate that you are grateful for the time and detailed information which will help you improve your service to him and other clients like him. Mention again that you will call within the next 90 days and schedule the call on your calendar.

Step 7:

If you go through steps 1 to 6 with four or five of your top clients, you will identify common areas where you fall short and where you need to focus. Start to implement changes in procedures, manpower, and whatever else is necessary to meet and exceed client expectation.

Step 8:

Within the next 90 days, call the client and say, "I want to thank you very much. We implemented certain changes based on the discussion I had with you." Then discuss the improvements employed to meet and exceed his or her expectations. Ask, "Is there anything else we need to do to meet and exceed your expectations?" At this point, most will say, "No, everything is fine."

Step 9:

From there, continue, "We want to build our client base with clients just like you and we want you as an advocate. We have identified two primary types of advocates. There are Referral Advocates, who refer us to at least one other person that is a friend or associate on a regular basis." You already know the person sitting across the table from you is not a Referral Advocate or a referral would have already been made. They are possibly a future Reference Advocate, but not a Referral Advocate. At this point, the client may get a little antsy. You say, "The other type of advocate is a Reference Advocate. That is someone who does not feel comfortable making a proactive introduction, but has no problem answering a few questions from a prospective client about what it is like to work with us. Which type of advocate are you?" Invariably, the client says, "I am the latter. I am a reference."

Step 10:

Because of the service you deliver, your client wants some way of repaying you and saying, "thank you." Advocacy provides that opportunity. Reiterate by saying, "If I run across a prospect that you do not know, you would not mind us setting up a call for you to talk to him or her and answer a few questions about what it is like to work with us?" "No, I wouldn't mind doing that." "Great. Thank you very much. I look forward to it." You build a list of

Reference Advocates by employing this process.

Applying Reference Advocates

The Reference Advocate list comes into play during the marketing process. After the introduction and profiling of the prospect, while building an asset allocation analysis and identifying the solution you want to deliver, have that prospect talk to two of your references. Proactively put them in contact with those people. I recommend that your team set up the call date and time between the advocate and your prospect while the prospect is in the profile meeting.

At the specified time your assistant first contacts the client on the phone and then calls the prospect. Once both are on the line and introduced, the assistant drops off the line and allows them to chat in private. This way you make sure the advocacy call happens.

When the prospect comes in for the closing presentation to hear the solution, he or she has already talked to two of your clients about what it is like to work with you. Often he or she is already "pre-sold" and will come in saying, "What do I have to do to sign up? I like what I heard." The solution has not even been presented, but the prospect is ready to commit. The Reference Advocate works because it introduces the prospect to the last part of the relationship model.

Head-Heart-Feet Relationship Model™

The relationship model is simple. Relationships are built by a head, heart, and feet exchange. You must first appeal to the head. You do that by showing you know what you are talking about and that you have expertise.

Secondly, the heart creates trust as you show that you are trustworthy. Thirdly, the feet are moved into action by actually delivering the goods. Most clients that have done business with you in the past did so without any real knowledge that you could deliver on your promises. By using references, you show you can and do deliver.

The advocacy luncheon is a major part of the Advocacy-Based Marketing System. It allows you to build off powerful relationships with your clients and then leverage as they introduce you to other people whom you invite to workshops, tele-classes, and seminars. I encourage you to try an advocacy luncheon in the near future.

First Conversation

All Relationships Start With a Conversation

The lost art of conversation is often replaced by meaningless fact finding and profiling. A real conversation with a client about their true assets can build the trust of a 20-year relationship in two hours and eliminate the need to prospect. We can grow our businesses exponentially when we understand why a client comes to see us, realize their unmet need, know their decision process, and focus our business on a unique client experience.

Setting Up The First Conversation

The client experience starts with the first contact. Continuity and consistency must be maintained throughout the entire relationship building process.

- Confirmation Letter
- Confirmation Call
- Meeting

First Call Script for the Communication Assistant

You have a name and then your assistant calls the prospect. By customizing the following script, he or she can establish an in-person appointment with the potential client:

"Mr. Jones, Bill Johnson asked that we contact you to set up an appointment. My name is Sally Smith. I am responsible for scheduling all appointments for the Investment Consulting Group. Is there a day next week that would be convenient for us to set an appointment with you?"

Confirmation Letter

[Date]

[Address Name]
[Position]
[Company]
[Address 1]
[Address 2]
[City], [State] [Zip]

Dear [Name]:

Just a note to confirm your appointment at our office on [Appointment Date] at [Appointment Time]. We are located at [Company Address]. [Company Directions] Thank you for reserving this time in your busy schedule for us. We look forward to this opportunity, [Salutation], to share with you information we feel will help you attain your goals. Please call our communication assistant, Patty at [Phone] if anything comes up that would require you to reschedule.

Sincerely,

[Signature]
[Title]

Confirmation Call Script

"Mr. Jones, this is Sally Smith of the Investment Consulting Group. I am calling to confirm your appointment with Joe Consultant for Monday, March 5th at 2:00 pm. If you have questions or need to reschedule, please give us a call back at 733-555-8800. Thank you."

All confirmation calls may be left on voice mail which does not require talking with the person.

The Normal Marketing Process

- Meet and Greet
- Profile
- Proposal
- Presentation
- Close

Every Appointment Creates The Next

Introduction

Scheduling appointments is a business necessity; it is the energy by which a business moves forward, yet this laborious activity is often avoided. Whether you handle scheduling yourself or delegate the task to an assistant, the activity is not enjoyable. Therefore the task is often delayed and business productivity suffers.

Would you like a process that guarantees every appointment is set without effort and no calls are needed to set appointments? Would you like to save time and effort in keeping your calendar full of valuable client appointments? Would you like to increase your productivity by focusing your time on what is most important?

If you answer in the affirmative, what happens when the answers are negative?

A Few Examples

When an appointment is not scheduled:
- The prospect referred to you becomes cold.
- An opportunity is missed because the client finds solutions elsewhere.
- A problem is allowed to fester into a crisis.
- Goodwill is lost because your answer to their concern is provided too slowly.
- Continuity and consistency are not maintained and your reputation suffers.
- You lose potential referrals.

How do we currently schedule appointments?

Every prospect starts in a process where the current appointment leads to their next appointment. Since you need to meet with a prospect several times before they become a client, keep the appointments close together to maintain the prospect's interest.

Once they become a client a business typically stops the process of scheduling the next appointment. The advisor waits for the client to call them or only calls when there is something to sell or discuss with the client. What was systematic becomes random. Our conversations focus on business and selling. Trust is not deepened and the relationship that was developing during initial meetings is stopped.

Since the client does not have a specific time scheduled to meet with you and deal with issues, they call with each individual question, wanting a quick answer. The number of incoming phone calls increases and, to avoid making a separate call, you try to use the time to sell or do other business while you have them on the phone. Before long the client hesitates to call, concerned that each call will lead to a sales pitch.

Such a waning process creates an adversarial relationship between the client and the business.

How can it change?

Continue scheduling the next appointment for the new prospect even after they become a client. Since they are already comfortable with the process of one appointment leading to the next, they will set a new next appointment even though it is a month, six months, or a year away. That starts the process.

Second, when you speak with your current clients schedule their next appointment. If you go through the process once with your entire client base they are scheduled for life.

Why would you want to change?

First, because it is easier to confirm an appointment than to schedule an appointment. No contact is required for a confirmation. You do not have to talk with the client. You can leave a voicemail or a message with an assistant. They can call you if they need to reschedule, otherwise the appointment is confirmed. The pressure of trying to connect with the client to schedule the appointment is avoided and more appointments can be confirmed in an hour than can be set.

Second, you avoid phone tag. Because a contact is required to schedule an appointment the biggest problem you have is that the client is rarely available when you call to arrange an appointment. Then you play phone tag trying to set the appointment.

Third, the calendar stays booked and no client or prospect slips through the cracks. Opportunities are not missed and you stay productive.

How does it work?

To begin, schedule all time off and team vacations on the calendar. Then all appointments can be scheduled for times when the team is wholly present.

Second, before a client or prospect leaves your office or a call ends, turn them over to your assistant to scheduled their next appointment. Just like at a dentist's office, a six-month checkup is scheduled today.

Even if they cannot confirm that the particular date is free while you are talking to them, select the date. Your office will call a week before to confirm and the meeting can be rescheduled at that time. This way an appointment is on the calendar regardless.

You may even give them a business card with the appointment details on the back. That way they can call you later that day, if the date will not work, and if the appointment will work they can post it directly to their own calendar. If you do not hear from them then the appointment is set and will be confirmed later.

Third, every Monday all appointments for the next week are confirmed, seven to twelve days in advance, without having to talk to the client. A voicemail can be left. This will require a time slot in the morning when appointment confirmations are handled. Everything is confirmed unless a client calls to reschedule.

Fourth, every day call and confirm the next day's appointments. This second confirmation call is made and left with voicemail, an assistant, or other contact.

By establishing a policy that every appointment creates the next appointment, and confirming a week in advance and the day before, you systematically stay in contact with all your clients and prospects and exceed their expectations.

Office Appointment Script:

"Ms. Smith, this is John from Susan Anderson's office calling to confirm your appointment next week with Susan at our office on Tuesday, July 3rd at 2 pm. If you need to reschedule please call me at 333-555-1234. Otherwise we look forward to seeing you Tuesday, July 3rd at 2:00 pm. Thank you."

Phone Appointment

"Ms. Smith, this is John from Susan Anderson's office calling to confirm your telephone appointment next week with Susan on Tuesday, July 3rd at 2 pm. If you need to reschedule please call me at 333-555-1234. Otherwise Susan looks forward to speaking with you Tuesday, July 3rd at 2:00 pm. Thank you."

For many of you a Virtual Assistant can handle the scheduling. I have used virtual assistants for scheduling for many years. See www.assistu.com for further information regarding virtual assistants.

Secrets of Successful Confirmation

Speak slowly and repeat the information twice.

New Office Policy

Every appointment creates the next appointment.

Uncover More Business With This Simple Script

If you can find out what's really on the minds of your clients and prospects, you are likely to unearth unexpected opportunities. Here's how a simple approach to opening productive dialogue can help.

How many times have you realized, mid-presentation, that you're losing your prospect's attention, that his mind seems to be drifting away from what you're saying? This is a common problem, particularly with new prospects. It's a problem you need to overcome since that initial interaction is pivotal in converting prospects to clients and setting the stage for a productive, long-lasting relationship.

A number of years ago, Kevin Daley wrote an outstanding book, *Socratic Selling: How to Ask the Questions That Get the Sale*. It contains extremely valuable information on opening conversations strategically in order to capture your prospect's attention. The following are the key points I've taken from what Daley calls the "Socratic Opening."

The power of a simple statement

If a client or prospect has trouble focusing on your presentation, he's probably preoccupied with an issue that supersedes your agenda. Your task, then, should be to draw out the issue that prevents him from giving you his full attention. Even more important, by encouraging him to talk about what's on his mind and then offering possible solutions, you'll add value to the relationship, build trust, and quickly convey your credibility and expertise.

Daley suggests using a specific conversation opener: "I am prepared, Mr. Jones, to talk about what we set this meeting up for today. However, before I begin, I would like to hear your thoughts so that I can focus my comments on what is most important to you." The statement is very simple yet also very powerful because it contains three parts that explain and set up your relationship with the prospect from this point forward.

1. "I am prepared . . ."

This first phrase lets your prospect know that you are ready with the necessary information for the meeting, that you have taken time to review his situation and that you understand what is at stake. It also impresses upon him that you are not interested in wasting time, neither his nor your own.

2. "But before I begin, I would like to hear your thoughts . . ."

This is one of the few cases when the use of "but" is acceptable in a conversation with a client or prospect. Typically, you should avoid using the words "but" or "however" since doing so may seem like you are taking issue with your prospect's previous remarks. Consider the following examples:

"I think that is a wonderful idea, but . . ."
"I understand your concerns, but . . ."
"I agree with you 100%, but . . ."

In each case using the word "and" instead of "but" would emphasize that you're understanding and connecting with the prospect rather than qualifying or undercutting his previous statement.

So why this use of "but"? When you say, "But before I begin...," you're simply interrupting yourself; your prospect hasn't spoken yet. In essence, you shift your focus away from yourself and toward him, to the fact that something important may be going on in his life that is occupying his thoughts. This issue may be more pressing than whatever was on his mind last week when you scheduled the meeting. If you continue with your planned agenda you will have a difficult time getting anywhere because he is bound to have trouble concentrating.

3. " . . . so I can focus my comments on what is most important to you."

Here, you send your prospect a message: what is important to him now may not be what was important to him when he originally scheduled the meeting, but that's alright. By letting you in on what he's thinking about, he opens the door for you to assist and service him at a higher level. What is important to him will become important to you.

A real-life example

Many years ago, just after reading Daley's book, I decided to use his approach during a particular Monday morning appointment. A CPA had referred us to a client with a small group retirement plan worth about $250,000 that experienced mismanagement in administration.

Proceeding with the Socratic Opening script, I said, "I am prepared to discuss your retirement plan today, but before I begin, let's hear your thoughts so I can focus my comments on what is most important to you."

Leaning back in his chair, the client admitted that his biggest problem right then was handling his mother-in-law's estate. "She made me the executor of her estate, and I have no idea what I'm doing. I am afraid that my wife and her two sisters are going to be upset with me for messing this up," he confessed.

At that point, I could have simply sympathized and continued with my presentation, but I don't think the client would have heard anything I said. Instead, I stopped and explained that we had dealt with a tremendous number of estate transfers over the last several years. I informed him that, if he'd give me just a few moments, I could give him a quick outline of the process and walk him through some of the steps and procedures.

What was supposed to be a thirty minute meeting turned into an hour and a half. He told his secretary to hold everything else while we made phone calls to the bank trust department and to the accountants and estate attorneys on our professional advisory board. We found answers to his questions, helped educate him on the process, and set up meetings so he could get all his issues resolved.

As I walked out the door he thanked me for my time. Then he added, "Oh, by the way, that retirement plan we were going to talk about but never got around to, just go ahead and send me the paperwork. You can take care of that also." The retirement plan was worth $250,000, and the estate was worth $8 million. Had we focused on the original agenda, I would have missed the opportunity.

The Four Differences Script

Incentive
- No Commission
- No Conflict of Interest
- We Sit on the Same Side of the Table

Performance
- Risk-Adjusted
- Always Reported Net

Reporting
- Quarterly Monitoring
- Profit & Loss, Not Just a Balance Sheet

Safety
- Due Diligence
- Monitoring
- Been Down the Path Before

One of the main objectives of your prospecting plan is to distinguish yourself from the herd of financial professionals. Probably, a big part of the reason you moved to fees was to do just that, to underscore for prospects your concern for them as individuals, letting them, in turn, see you as an individual they can trust. The Four Differences script can win prospects by putting the strongest features of your fee-based strategy up front. Use this advantage to separate yourself from the herd.

The "Four Differences" Script

"Mr. Jones, we are investment management consultants. There are four major differences between what we do as consultants and what your broker, banker, financial planner, insurance agent, or other financial professional has done for you. These four differences separate us from the rest of the financial services industry."

Same Side Of The Table

"The first difference is the incentive.

We charge no commissions on any of our managed accounts. We believe there is a conflict of interest between commission and a client's best interest. When your broker calls you up and tells you to buy XYZ and you do, he makes a commission. Six months later, he may call you back and say that it is time to sell XYZ. You sell it and he gets paid again. This is a win-win proposition for the broker, but for you it could go either way; you either make money or you lose money. We believe that is unfair and constitutes a conflict of interest. For this reason, as consultants, we have established our revenue stream so that we win or lose with you.

The way we do that is by charging a fee as a percentage of your total assets under management. If your account is growing, we are both making money. The reverse is true as well. If your account is losing money, we are losing revenue too. In this way we are winning and losing together. We believe that this is a fair arrangement in that our incentive is the same as yours. We are looking at your assets from the same side of the table, from the same perspective. We want the assets to grow and continue to be safe just as you do."

Risk Adjustments

"Incentive is the first difference. Performance is the second.

When you talk about performance, most people talk

about the rate of return. This refers to what investment return you made last year, 'I made 8%, 12%, or 15%.' But we refer to "risk-adjusted performance." It does not make any difference how much you made last year if you do not take risk into account. Two managers could have both made 15% last year, but without knowing how much risk each manager took you do not know if 15% was a good or bad return.

For this reason, we assess all performance on a risk-adjusted basis, both in terms of the managers and total portfolio returns. Our code of ethics requires us to quote performance numbers on a net/net basis. That means after all costs have been accounted for so you know exactly what you have made. A broker can call you up and say that the stock you bought at $10 is now at $12 so that you are up 20%. You know that does not sound right when you paid 75 cents to buy the stock and you will have to pay 75 cents to sell it. As consultants we are required to say that at the sell your $10 stock purchase was up 5% net of all costs, which is substantially different than being up 20%. With risk-adjusted performance we can assess how much risk is taken for the performance we receive."

Complete Records

"To this point the differences are incentive and performance. The third difference is reporting.

I am amazed at the number of executives who would never consider running their businesses without a balance sheet, a P&L, and a cash-flow statement, yet they are satisfied to run their personal and corporate finances on nothing more than the monthly balance sheet they receive from their brokerage firm, mutual fund company, or bank.

I believe that the monthly statement is inadequate. Therefore, every 90 days, we will send you a progress report. The quarterly report will include a balance sheet, Profit and Loss statement, and a cash-flow summary. It will allow you to make business decisions about your personal and corporate assets; to understand your current financial position and see your future resources. Also, as part of the reporting, and in addition to your regular quarterly progress report, we will provide realized gain and loss statements at the end of each year for tax purposes. I believe these reporting tools will give you the information necessary to make intelligent, informed decisions concerning your assets."

Personal Security

"The first difference is incentive, the second is performance, the third is reporting, and the fourth and final difference is safety.

Beyond the safety provided by the due-diligence process, whereby we scrutinize both the independent money managers and ourselves, as consultants we address safety regarding your lifestyle and the uncertain future. Though you are older than I am, I have already seen the remainder of your life circumstances through the lives of other clients. I have been down that path over and over. I have gone through the estate transfer of wealth from one generation to the next many times. In that process, I learned where you need to turn right and where you need to turn left. The life in front of you is a maze. I have been through the maze time and again.

A further safety factor is that we can show you how the goals and objectives you establish for your family can be maintained in your absence. The objectives you establish can be set forth and the family can be taken care of into the next generation. We are concerned with the safety of the immediate principal and the safety of the next generations.

To recap, the differences we offer are in incentive, performance, reporting, and last and most importantly, safety.

Does it make sense?"

The Four Differences Script facilitates a successful first introduction to you and your team. It says what your prospects and clients believe, but have never heard before. The script sets you apart.

The Movie Theater

Why do our clients and prospects come to see us? This is a simple question that is rarely asked and often misunderstood. Throughout my coaching and consulting I have asked this question to teams and am always surprised how few understand why people really come to see them. Ask yourself this question and over the following pages we will elaborate further.

Role Play

What goes on when a prospect walks into our office? Take a moment and replay the last several appointments in your mind.

Little Red Wagon Script™

The following script was previously only available to my coaching clients. My coaching clients have tremendous success with this script and use it to separate themselves from the multitude of investment consultants in their marketplace.

The Little Red Wagon Script™ was developed from a number of personal conversations in which consultants said, "I like the Exponential Relationship concept and the use of the Exponential Relationship Conversation has changed my client relationships, but I have a difficult time explaining to clients why I'm talking to them about their life and not about their money."

Perhaps many of you have dealt with similar explanations. How do you have a two-hour conversation with a client about their past and future life plans and steer them away from talking about their portfolio or investments? The Little Red Wagon Script™ was created to assist you in that endeavor.

Getting Started

The Little Red Wagon Script™ was designed to be delivered live. It is possible to convey over the phone, but is fashioned as a visual message. I encourage you to buy a Radio Flyer wagon. By visiting the Radio Flyer website at www.radioflyer.com, you can see all sizes available and sizes you can bring into your office. Next, you need a 12-inch wall clock, one with a large display and big hands. Lastly, purchase a couple of empty money bags from your local bank. Fill these with whatever gives the illusion of them being full. These three props provide the visual aids for The Little Red Wagon Script™.

The Script

"Mr. & Mrs. Jones, it is my pleasure to meet with you today. I'd like to take a moment to explain something I've experienced that has changed and more importantly modified the way I work with clients. I've been astounded over the last three years at the number of clients and prospects that have been devastated in the marketplace. As a result of the decline in the stock market they have been hurt financially and otherwise, and it has reiterated to us the importance of understanding our client's needs. We believe the reason these individuals suffered in the market was because no one took time up front to genuinely understand them. They were given solutions, but no one took time to perform the diagnosis and examination necessary to make certain the prescriptions written were the correct remedies.

I realize, when you walked into this office today, you came in with two assets and two resources. The two assets you brought with you are your relationships and your well-being. If you ask someone on his deathbed what is most important to him, typically he wishes he built deeper relationships with the ones he loved and that he spent more time focusing on his health. What he wants is better health and to have had better relationships. Given that, we believe every client places high importance and value on these two assets – relationships and well-being. The life energy that makes up your health and the relationships around you are the internal and external components of your life. Those are most important.

You also brought in a little red wagon with you today. (At this point bring out your red wagon with the props inside.) Your resources are in this wagon. You probably didn't realize you brought in a wagon, but you did. Everybody who comes to see us brings it with them and it holds the two things that are your tools and resources for life. First is your time (you pick up the clock) and the second is your money (show them the money bags).

Normally, if you go to the average consultant in the financial services industry, he or she takes the little red wagon, sticks the money bags on top of the table, and talks about money. Why do they do this? They don't realize the money is nothing but a resource. It's like time. It's only a tool you have to enhance the two most important things in your life – your relationships and your well-being. Your money is simply a tool that can help you have a better life. For some reason, the financial services industry has operated under the assumption that money is an asset, but it's not. Money is a tool.

We will put the tools, the money and time, back in the red wagon and place it back in the corner of the room. We leave it there because we need to understand who you are, what is important to you, what you see as challenges in your life, the opportunities you want to pursue, where you are today, and where you want to go. We need to understand the purpose and drive you had while you worked to amass this money. Until we understand your life, it would be meaningless for us to try to figure out what to do with the tools and resources you have in the little red wagon. We will park your red wagon in the corner until both you and I understand and agree exactly where you are and where you want to go. Does that make sense, Mr. & Mrs. Jones?"

Why it Works

At this point, you may be thinking that this is the hokiest thing you ever heard, but, I promise you, it works. One of my most successful coaching clients tried it for a few months with 10 of his top clients and he was amazed with the results. With this script and the visual aids your clients cannot miss the point. You are telling them money is not important, their life is. The reason they had problems in the past was because their advisor focused on their money and not on their client's life. Nobody misses that point. The visual aids make it perfectly clear.

The visual aids also make it clear to you and help you remember where to keep the focus. Your focus needs to be on the client's life, not on the money.

Add the Little Red Wagon Script™ to the front end of your relationship conversation. If you take the time to buy the red wagon, the clock, and money bags, I think you will find you can clearly explain what separates you from the other people in your industry and your community. Your clients will know immediately that your focus is different than anybody else they ever talked to and it eliminates the need for you to keep answering the question, "When are we going to talk about the money?" You aren't going to talk about the money until you understand the life.

The Lost Art of Conversation

In our endeavor to move quickly toward closing the sale, we have lost the art of conversation. The loss is driven by our focus on the solicitation model, which businesses have focused on since the late 1970's. For 25 years business has been in "solicitation mode" because, for 25 years, our customers have been in "buy mode". Trust was not a primary issue for customers; they sought information in order to make intelligent buying decisions. Time has changed things. Due to the loss of trust in accountants, lawyers, stock brokers, and corporate officers, consumers made a change from 2000 to 2002 and trust rose to the top of their agendas.

Since trust precedes action, consumers will not act until they trust, which relates to a previous section about the connection between the Head, Heart, and Feet. To refresh, all relationship building starts in the head (expertise), then proceeds to the heart (trust), and finally to the feet (action). Therefore, we must first concentrate on building trust because client action follows.

Our problem with conversation begins with how we view the entire client encounter. Let's start with their first entrance into our office. Ask yourself, what is a client looking for when he or she visits you? Your response may include advice, help with investments, performance, proper asset allocation, manager selection, financial planning, wealth management, or service. Therein lies the problem. From the beginning we, as an industry, do not understand our relationship with the client.

Clients walk into our office with two assets and two resources. Their assets are the relationships in their life and their personal well-being. These are the two assets valued most when on their deathbed. The resources they bring with them are time and money. The financial services industry has tried to make people believe that money is an asset, but clients know that it is only a tool to be used to improve their relationships and energy.

Every prospect and client enters your office pulling a little red wagon full of time and money. They look for our help and then wonder why we jump in the wagon and start playing with the money. Because this has been their experience with every financial professional they have almost given up trying to find someone to meet their real need.

And what is this real need? They want to deepen the relationships around them and have more energy, i.e. health. These allow our client to enjoy the life they see in their future to the fullest. We can manage energy and relationships because they are renewable. I recommend you read the book *The Power of Full Engagement* by Jim Loehr and Tony Schwartz.

Another outstanding book is *The Experience Economy* by Joseph Pine and James Gilmore. Pine and Gilmore explain why clients are looking for an experience. They describe the business experience as a stage with the performance side in front of the curtain and the production side behind the curtain. Behind the curtain are the lights, props, and sound - the tools and resources you have for your industry like your team, service, systems, products, and technology. These are typically the things businesses talk about when asked, "Why should we work with you?" But these are not the reasons a person goes to the theater. A person does not want to see how the props are moved around. The production side needs to be hidden. The client wants to see what happens in front of the curtain, what happens on stage, or on the movie screen. Too often we put the back stage functions on front stage and ask the client to enjoy the show as we talk on and on about our products and services.

What does the client want to see on stage? A performance. But a performance of what? Not us, a performance of life - their life lived out into the future. They did not come in to see us play with the little red wagon full of money that comes with their life. Our clients want to see a new vision of their life lived out through retirement. They want to conceive a hopeful future. They want to believe there is a course of action they can take to achieve that reality.

Charles Allen said, "Anything the mind can conceive and believe, it can achieve." It is our responsibility to help our clients conceive their future, believe in its possibility, and set a course of action to achieve that reality.

The Laws of Conversation

Ask

Ask an open-ended question about the person, not their money.

Listen

Listen, really listen, to their answer. (Do not think about the next question, just listen.)

Pause

Your next question is embedded in the client's answer to your previous question. (Do not worry about the "pregnant pause", you will know what to ask next by what they talk about.)

Focus

Stay focused on the person. Never mention money, your business, or anything that benefits you.

Continue

Continue to listen for the emotional answer that reveals the feelings behind the facts.

Important Final Step

At the end of the conversation you should know the following about your client:

- Thinker vs. Feeler
- Past vs. Future
- Fear vs. Hope
- Motivators
- Unmet Need
- Decision Process

At the end of the conversation you should be able to answer the following questions:

- What is the current **purpose** of their life?
- What are the biggest **challenges** they face?
- What are the **opportunities** they could pursue if the challenges were removed?
- Where are they **today** in their life?
- Where do they want to be in **twenty years**?
- What **motivates** the actions of their life?
- Do they have an **unmet need** that is holding them back from making decisions?
- What is their **decision process**?

If you cannot answer these questions you have a lot of facts about the client, but not the motivations and reasons behind the facts. People do not make decisions based upon facts. Action is propelled by emotions. Remember, head, heart, then feet.

PRESENTATION

A Strategic Meeting

The Unmet Needs revealed in the Relationship Conversation become the raw material for a creative solution. The delivery of the solution must be a Unique Experience.

Checklist for Presentation Meeting

- Client drink preference
- Presentation materials
- Focus on the female partner
- Stand to educate and sit to relate
- Keep the presentation short
- Spend extra time answering questions

ROI vs. ROR

During difficult times, it is important that your clients understand their return on investment (ROI), but, contrary to usual thinking, I do not mean their monetary investment in this case. Your clients need to understand the investment they have made in a relationship with you and your team. It is return on the time, effort, and energy put into the process called fee-based managed money. I call this Return on Relationship™ (ROR).

It is important that you introduce this concept early. During the profiling process, go through a series of questions to identify expectations the client has regarding your relationship. When does the client want to retire? How much do they need to live on during retirement? What travel budget do they want to maintain? What college funding is needed? What is their current budget? The answers to these and other questions establish how they want their life to be managed and, in essence, establishes the benchmarks against which you can be measured.

On an annual basis, or whenever the relationship is at risk, you can refer back to these questions and record them on the Return on Relationship™ Worksheet.

To set up this worksheet create three columns. In the first column, make a list of the client's key criteria such as retirement date, retirement age, retirement income, travel budget, etc.

In the middle column, write the benchmarks the client supplied in the initial profiling process. For instance, if the client said he wanted to retire at age 65, that number goes in the middle column beside retirement age.

The third column is for current information. As you complete the worksheet you can say, "Mr. Jones, you initially told us you wanted to retire at age 65, but, currently, you are on target to retire at age 62." Write that number in the final column. "And, Mr. Jones, you wanted to retire in 2012, but you are able to retire in 2009, correct? You told us that you wanted to retire with $100,000 annual income, but now you are on track to build a $120,000 plus income per year."

As you go through the list, continue to write current values in the third column. "You wanted a $10,000 annual travel budget, but we gave you $25,000 annually the last couple of years. You wanted to educate your children, which has been done. You wanted monthly communication from us, which we provided." Continue on through the list.

Illustrating the Return on Relationship™ is critical to retaining clients in a difficult markets. By going through the process, asking the questions early in the relationship, then documenting answers, you have a Return on Relationship™ analysis tool.

The Investment Process

My team defined our investment process as "a disciplined approach to making investment decisions by providing objective information and counsel to help clients attain their personal and financial goals."

Create a statement that defines your investment process. This statement should build confidence and clearly express your primary investment focus.

The Four Decisions

Four decisions need to be made to invest client money properly:

Risk Profile - Client decides
Holding Period - Client decides
Asset Allocation - Advisor decides
Manager Selection - Advisor decides

We need to remind our clients that Consulting is a partnership. Only the client knows their risk profile and holding period for the money and when they change. Only the consultant knows the proper asset mix and managers for a client's particular risk profile. Advisors need to incorporate clients into the Investment Process and not make assumptions about the client's risk tolerance.

Four Stages of Consulting

The Presentation

Throughout my career I used Frontier Analytic's Allocation Master for presentations to clients. Though the team maintained other institutional software optimization tools, Allocation Master had the best client presentation. The following are the concepts I focused on during a client presentation:

There seems to be a problem...

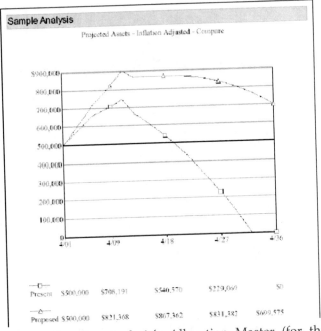

Source: Frontier Analytic's Allocation Master (for the latest version go to www.allocationmaster.com)

Everything is fine as long as the client dies early. Too often clients do not have a clear perspective on the amount of money necessary for retirement. Retirement funding must be illustrated in the beginning.

The assets need to be reallocated...

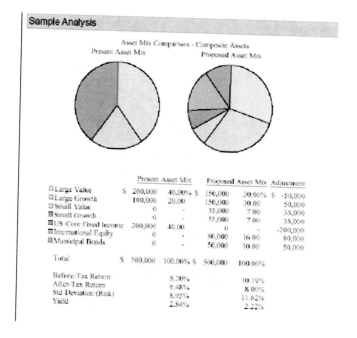

Sample Analysis

Asset Mix Comparison - Composite Assets

Present Asset Mix — Proposed Asset Mix

		Present Asset Mix		Proposed Asset Mix		Adjustment
☐ Large Value	S	200,000	40.00%	S 150,000	30.00%	S -50,000
☐ Large Growth		100,000	20.00	150,000	30.00	50,000
☐ Small Value		0	-	35,000	7.00	35,000
■ Small Growth		0	-	35,000	7.00	35,000
■ US Core Fixed Income		200,000	40.00	0	-	-200,000
■ International Equity		0	-	80,000	16.00	80,000
■ Municipal Bonds		0	-	50,000	10.00	50,000
Total	S	500,000	100.00%	S 500,000	100.00%	
Before-Tax Return			8.70%		10.19%	
After-Tax Return			8.48%		8.00%	
Std Deviation (Risk)			8.95%		11.62%	
Yield			2.84%		2.22%	

Source: Frontier Analytic's Allocation Master (for the latest version go to www.allocationmaster.com)

The most important decision that must be made during this presentation is the necessity of moving from the present misallocated portfolio to the proposed proper asset allocation.

The proper mix for you now...

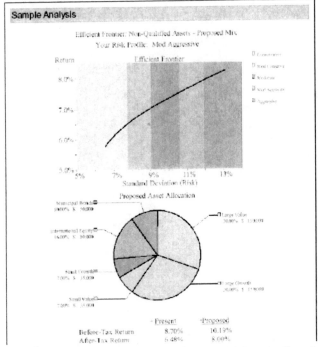

Source: Frontier Analytic's Allocation Master (for the
latest version go to www.allocationmaster.com)

Take the time to explain where this pie chart comes from
and how it adjusts over time as the client's risk profile
changes.

Long and short-term historical...

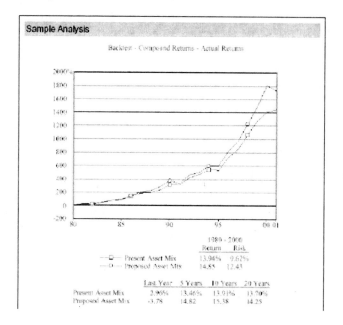

Source: Frontier Analytic's Allocation Master (for the latest version go to www.allocationmaster.com)

Examine the difference between long and short-term performance.

Short-term managed...

CDA Hypothetical

Multiple Fund Composite

- $30,000 initial investment in Enterprise Growth Portfolio A on 12/31/90 which was subject to an annual advisory fee of 1.20%.
- $30,000 initial investment in PriceCT. Equity Income on 12/31/90 which was subject to an annual advisory fee of 1.20%.
- $20,000 initial investment in Putnam New Opportunities A on 12/31/90 which was subject to an annual advisory fee of 1.20%.
- $20,000 initial investment in Templeton Foreign I on 12/31/90 which was subject to an annual advisory fee of 1.20%.

Prepared for : MODERATE GROWTH MODEL
Requested by : Investment Consulting Group
Prepared by : Interstate/Johnson Lane
Atlanta, GA 30326

Month			Cash Flows and Outflows				Holdings
				Dividends			
End	Invest	Withdrawal	Income	Capital Gains	Reinvest	Taxes Due	Market Value
12/90	100,000						100,000
12/91	0	0	2,490	5,248	7,738	-	135,638
12/92	0	0	2,208	6,711	8,919	-	152,282
12/93	0	0	1,917	6,322	8,239	-	180,932
12/94	0	0	2,228	6,919	9,145	-	182,318
12/95	0	0	2,907	5,513	8,421	-	243,514
12/96	0	0	3,145	8,694	11,839	-	289,260
12/97	0	0	5,803	13,033	18,837	-	356,563
03/98	0	0	526	488	1,014	-	398,502
Total	100,000	0	21,222	52,930	74,152	-	

	Mkt Val
Ending Amount Attributable to Principal :	207,801
Income :	18,293
Capital Gain :	72,408
Total Ending Amount :	398,502
Average Annual Return on the Account :	21.01%

Source: CDA HySales

Calculate the managed return, net of all expenses.

Three types of performance...

Long-Term Historical	Short-Term Historical	Managed
10.19%	15.38%	21.01%
75 years	10 years	10 years

As the client records the three types of performance on a separate sheet, they are able to clearly see that long-term forecasting cannot be based on short-term performance. The decision concerns properly allocating the assets for the future.

Closing Statement

Thinkers: Does this make sense?
Feelers: Are you comfortable with this?

HANDLING OBJECTIONS

Backfilling Information

> *Expertise is established in the dialogue that occurs during the question and answer session.*

Question vs. Objection

There is a difference between a question and an objection. A question is simply a request for information or for a reply. An objection, however, is a feeling or expression of opposition and identifies potential disagreement. When making a presentation to a client or prospect for the first time, the client or prospect naturally has questions. It is important for you to realize the difference between a question and an objection.

The best way to handle both is to answer them in your presentation. The client understands the answer now in it's larger context. Agreement now makes disagreement later unnecessary. If you do not successfully handle the objection up front, you will either not get the business or, if you do, you may not keep it.

Sample Objections

The following are typical objections voiced by clients against managed money along with my best responses for addressing their concerns:

Why would I want to move to managed money; isn't what we have been doing good enough?

"Mr. Jones, over the last several years, technology changed dramatically. New pricing structures and advantages have come to the table that did not exist in the past. To give you an example, in the past, when we wanted to invest your money, we found a family of mutual funds that had a good track record, stable manager mix, and the ability to make transfers among that family of funds at no cost. That was the best possible recommendation we could make to you at the time. Today, however, with better technology, we can recommend multiple fund families within the same account. In any given fund family, the managers are typically great at managing one asset class, but not as strong in every asset class. They might be a great big-cap, growth manager, but less capable at value stocks, small-cap, international, or other assets classes. Today we can identify what your asset allocation should be based upon your current circumstances and then identify the best possible manager in each asset class, regardless of the fund family and without worrying about exchange fees. In addition, as your circumstances and your risk profile change over time, we can adapt and keep your portfolio in proper allocation.

The pricing structures have also changed and now there are institutional-priced investment vehicles available to you. In the past, you had to have millions of dollars to invest in these funds, but our firm's buying power enables you to take advantage of an institutional pricing structure. These changes opened new doors of opportunity for us to better manage your assets. Lower costs and the ability to truly diversify your portfolio are compelling reasons to look at managed money as an alternative."

Will I pay a lot when I convert to the new managed money program? Will it cost a lot in taxes to make this transition?

"Mr. Jones, I do not believe it will, but to make certain we will run a break-even analysis for you.

There is a common misconception concerning capital gains

in that many people believe they will pay taxes on their entire asset base. That is not the case. Capital gains have been paid every year on the funds you own. Typically, rather than owing 20% of the total in taxes, taxes are 5% or less of the total value. In many cases, particularly if you invested in B-shares where expense ratios can be 2% or more, the break-even analysis can be a short period of time. Because institutional funds do not have the higher expense ratios and their net performance is much better than B-share funds, short break-even periods apply. For a portfolio of individual stocks there are other factors to consider in the break-even analysis.

Often you will find an un-diversified portfolio. The portfolio does not include the other asset classes necessary to protect it on the downside, which can create tremendous problems. Consider, for instance, some of the great companies like IBM, Coca Cola, and Kodak; they dropped substantially, more than 20% in a one-year period of time. If you diversified a portion of those assets you would have paid 20% in capital gains on the appreciation, but avoided the 40-50% loss in real principle that would have occurred when the market corrected. If you think there is a potential for greater than 20% correction in the stocks you own there is an overwhelming reason to look at diversifying those assets into a mix of asset classes. When the market pulls back, they will have a lower downside risk than the individual securities you own."

Can I get an income from my managed account?

"Yes, you can, Mr. Jones. There is a perception among the investing community that the only way to get income is to buy bonds, but that is a misconception. It is also a common belief that a person should be a growth investor until retirement at which time they should become an income investor for their remaining years. That may have been true at one time, when people only lived a few years past retirement, but nowadays life expectancy extends twenty or thirty years later. Inflation will have an impact on those retirement years. For that reason we believe a client should always be a growth investor. It is important to understand that not only is there a need to offset inflation there is also a tax difference between investing in bonds and stocks. What you have available to spend is the buying power of your money after inflation. Therefore, when you look at a CD portfolio, which continuously lost money after tax and inflation over the last 15 years, versus a stock portfolio, which has continually made a positive rate of return, one vehicle is truly safer than the other. This is particularly true in preserving buying power.

Let's go back to the question of income. Suppose we have two investors, one is a stock investor and the other invests in bonds. It does not make a difference whether those are tax-free bonds or taxable bonds; the net return is the same. They both take $100,000 out of their portfolio on a pre-tax basis. The stock investor pays 20% capital gains and the bond investor pays 39% in taxes. Net/net, the stock investor ends up with more money because he paid almost 45% less in taxes. His investment will outpace inflation. I believe you will see that receiving income through a stock portfolio makes more sense."

Why not just buy big-cap, growth stocks* since they have performed well for the last 3 years?

*applies to any asset class that outperforms for a period

"I agree that big-cap, growth stocks had outstanding performance over the last several years. That is a compelling reason to own them in your portfolio, but they need to be part of the overall mix. If you compare large-cap growth versus large-cap value stocks over a long period, fifteen years or so, they will have an average return that is almost identical. There is less than a tenth of a percent difference between the two styles. However, if you look at any single year there is a substantial difference, sometimes a double digit difference in return. Therefore, to take advantage of all benefits both large-cap growth and large-cap value offer, we recommend that a client split their large-cap position fifty-fifty between growth and value. This ensures we do not bet on which of the two asset classes will outperform over the next period. We don't want to try timing the market by moving back and forth between the two classes. Investing in an asset class when it is out of favor can adversely affect the portfolio, whereas, over the long-term, the actual return of the two is still outstanding.

Mr. Jones, though large-cap growth has been in favor for the last several years, there is a parallel period which bears examination. If you look back at the three-year period from 1989 to 1991, large-cap growth substantially outperformed value stocks. Along came 1992 and large-cap growth underperformed large-cap value, so much so that large-cap managers lost all the relative value they added over the previous three years. If you had a portfolio equally divided between large-value managers and large-growth managers, you had a substantially better four-year performance than you would have holding the large-growth manager alone. The same thing happened in the period from 1995 to 1999. Again, growth stocks outperformed, but then lost all outperformance over the next two years. This is the reason we believe in asset allocation and diversifying among asset classes."

Managed futures scare me.

"Mr. Jones, managed futures can be daunting. For that reason, I would like to explain the type of futures we use. There are two major types of futures investments which are defined by whether or not you own an underlying asset. The first type of futures investor is one who owns the underlying asset. For example, the person who owns orange groves in Florida will buy orange juice futures, someone who owns a large wheat field in Kansas will buy grain futures, and the bank with a large bond portfolio might purchase interest rate futures. These type of investors are called hedgers; they use a conservative strategy of hedging their underlying assets, which they own in the futures market. A hedging strategy works much like an insurance policy because it protects the assets you have. This is a conservative investment and one many institutions employ. The second type of futures investor is someone who does not own the underlying assets; they do not own orange groves, wheat fields, or bonds. They buy the future itself on speculation. This is an extremely aggressive investment strategy and it is estimated that about 95% of such investors lose their entire principal over an 18-month period. We have never participated in this type of futures investing, nor will we.

We have established a relationship with XYZ, one of the largest futures fund managers. We set up a portfolio to hedge 90% of the assets we own. Within a client's total portfolio, 90% is invested in the market through stocks and bonds; the remaining 10% is placed in managed futures. The futures portion protects the other 90% against the volatility of those assets. Historically, the strategy has proved prudent during periods of tremendous downside volatility. It works in much the same way a seesaw works. When the 90% is down, the 10% tends to be up. When the 90% is up, the 10% tends to be flat or down. In many years, the 10% investment in the futures fund allowed us to maintain a positive return for a year in which the markets substantially underperformed."

If I do what you ask, I will be hit with a back-end redemption fee (or capital gain) and will have less money to invest. Why is this a good idea?

Both the back-end load and the capital gain issue are essentially the same question. The client says, "I have X dollars today, but if I do what you recommend and move to fee-based business, I will have less money tomorrow to reinvest."

First, we must deal with the capital gain issue. The client assumes they will pay 100% of the capital gains tax. In other words, for the United States, the client will pay 20% on the total investment and in Canada they would pay 25% of the total investment. That is virtually never the case. Each scenario would require a zero cost basis on their investment portfolio, which rarely exists.

Understand the capital gain issue by realizing you think one number and your client thinks another, higher number. First, calculate the actual capital gain. In most cases, with mutual funds and the like, the capital gain works out to around 5% of the total investment, substantially less than the 20% or 25% the client assumes they must pay. Presented with this calculation alone, the client often says, "Oh, I had no idea it would be that low. No problem. Let's do it."

Subsequently, address the back-end load, which in most cases is a declining redemption starting around 5% and declining to 0% over time. Again, the client has 100% of his assets or $100 for example and if the recommendation is implemented his assets will immediately decline to $95. A break-even analysis is required to calculate the forward rate of return of the current investment portfolio and a forward rate of return on the future investment. Make these net return figures, net of all expenses, management fees, and internal costs so you have net/net returns comparing apples to apples. Then calculate time. When do the two lines cross? Where is the break-even point? If the break-even is a short enough period of time, it is prudent to make the investment change. It is economically viable. For most clients, an 18 to 24 month break-even is fairly insignificant relative to the long-term growth of the portfolio.

In answer to the client's objections, compute the calculation, identify the forward rate of return for both scenarios, calculate the time necessary to get to a break-even, and then, by your integrity and the individual situation of the client, determine whether it is an economically viable move. By educating your client you will almost always overcome the objection.

Why should we change what we are doing? You are buying stocks for me, which has worked well, and I like working with you.

"Mr. Jones, imagine for a moment you were just made the custodian of a $5 billion trust. Would you go to a local stockbroker, like myself, then between the two of us, decide upon 25 to 30 different stocks and manage the $5 billion that way? Your answer is probably, "No." You would do what institutions have done for decades. You would hire a consultant who would identify your risk profile, determine the holding period for the money, run an asset allocation analysis, and select managers that match the needs of the portfolio and the objectives of the funds. Your consultant would monitor managers and, when necessary, recommend firing and replacing one or more of those managers. That is what you would do with $5 billion. If technology today allows us to do with $500,000 what could only be done with $5 billion in the past, shouldn't you take advantage of it?"

The market is going down and fluctuating too much for me to invest right now.

"Mr. Jones, the markets are volatile in both directions, up and down. We understand that each client has a specific risk profile at specific points in his or her life. For this reason, it is important to run our Risk Profile Analysis to identify exactly where you are on the risk spectrum. Then we build an appropriate portfolio which reduces the impact of market volitility on your assets. This enables you to continue participating in the market. Converting assets to cash is not an alternative; after tax and after inflation, cash has always lost money over a 15 year, or longer, period. You cannot afford to have the purchasing power of your money remain stagnant or decline."

I already have a broker and he doesn't charge me a 1% fee.

"Yes, Mr. Jones, you have a broker and he does not charge you a fee, nor does he offer the services we offer. Stockbrokers are suitable for smaller clients who don't have the assets necessary to participate in professional fee-based business. Like institutions that don't hire stockbrokers to manage their investments, you should hire money managers and a consultant. You have a larger pool of assets and available technology allows us to offer you a Risk Profile Analysis, a Holding Period Analysis, and a proper Asset Allocation Analysis, along with proper manager selection and ongoing monitoring.

In the end, what you think you pay as a fee doesn't really cost you anything. Factor in the advantages, beginning with the Manager Advantage. By hiring the manager through our firm you save a minimum of 0.5%. If you dealt with the manager directly they would charge you 1%. They charge us 0.5% because of our buying power in the industry. Second is the Rebalancing Advantage. Since we rebalance the portfolio every year there is more than a 1% advantage. By selling out of an asset class at a high and reinvesting into another asset class that is low, the differential adds about 1% per year to the portfolio over time. The third advantage is the advantage my team and I offer. We continually monitor your managers and will fire those that change in their makeup in a way that could adversely affect performance. We monitor the markets and make asset class exchanges when necessary. We make these changes on an annual basis and have added on average at least 1% advantage to portfolios under management. Though you pay 2% in fees, we add 2.5% or more in value each year. Your broker, who does not charge fees, does not provide these services and advantages."

How do I know the investments you select will do better than those I can buy on my own?

"Morningstar ran a survey of 218 growth funds and their performance over a 5-year period ending in 1995. On average the funds compounded a 12.2% return. The investors in those funds compounded a -2.2% return for the same period.

Investors assume they are substantially smarter than professionals and do not do what the average investor does. That is why we have the average investor. Most investors allow their emotions to get involved. They become attached to decisions. As consultants, we stay detached, stay objective, and look out for what is in your best interest because our fee is based upon being paid the same way you are. If your assets are declining in value, we lose money as you do. As your assets increase in value, our revenue increases. We have an incentive to ensure the investment choices we make are for your benefit."

The bank trust department will manage my money for 1.25% or I can go directly to the money manager. Why should I hire you as a consultant?

"Mr. Jones, will a trust department or money manager or, for that matter, your individual stockbroker tell you, "I am not doing well as a manager of your money anymore and I think you should fire me."? As a consultant, we are like a general contractor. We work with subcontractors, the money managers in different fields, and diversify your assets over multiple managers and multiple asset classes.

When the painter messes up, the general contractor fires the painter and replaces him with another painter. But when the bank department messes up and does not do a good job, they do not fire themselves. That is why you need an investment management consultant, an objective party to look out for your best interest and tell you when it is necessary to fire that subcontractor."

I am tired of losing money. With the market in recession, I am not sure I want to invest in stocks.

"There has never been a 15 year period when, after tax and after inflation, stocks have had a negative return. In almost every 15 year period in history, fixed income and cash have lost money after tax and inflation. The question concerns extending the perspective beyond the short-term perspective. The only time you stop investing in business and stop investing in the market is when you contemplate the future and believe that 25 years from now we will no longer cure diseases, 25 years from now we will not have better health care, 25 years from now we will not have better technology or faster computers, and 25 years from now the whole world will be worse off than it is today. If you believe that then, yes, you should stop buying stocks. If you contemplate the future and see hope, you see a horizon that proffers better technology, better medical services, better means of communication, then, yes, you want to be an investor. Stocks are your way of participating."

Your fee is higher than the one I pay for mutual funds and you have a smaller support staff. Why should I pay more?

"Mr. Jones, the mutual fund is a portfolio designed for every person, for any person, for the average investor. What we do is similar to your private banker; we specialize. We specialize in high net worth individuals who have specific needs. We do not deal with a rigid design for the average investor with $5,000 who fits into a pool without something customized to his needs. We are a specialized team designed to focus on a select group of clients and their specific needs. We help clients identify those needs by doing the profiling necessary to understand the client at a deeper level and bear the answers in mind to build a solution that specifically meets our client's needs. We are able to do tax-loss selling at the end of each year, what we call capturing the tax advantages inside the portfolio. We create portfolios to meet the needs of clients, restrict certain investments the client does not want to invest in, and customize. Mutual funds cannot accomplish such tasks."

I tried paying by fees before and ended up paying to be ignored. I would rather pay when I do a trade.

"Mr. Jones, this is not an issue of fees. This is an issue of bad consulting, an issue where the team had more interest in themselves than you. I am happy to provide the names of a few of our clients who will certainly tell you we do not ignore our clients. We have systems in place to help us understand you at a deeper level. We spend time trying to understand who you are, why you are here, what purpose the funds in your life have, what the legacy you want to leave behind involves, what challenges you see ahead of you, the opportunities you could focus on, where you are now, and where you want to be. By concentrating on these factors, we will be able to meet your needs.

We are specialists that focus on a small, select group of clients and attend to them. I am sorry you had a negative experience, but not every consultant is that way. Just as there are bad businesses in every industry, that is not the industry as a whole. I believe, if you take time to talk to some of our clients, you will find we are substantially different than the consulting you have experienced in the past."

I don't like switching around my investments all the time. I have investments I want to keep, like stocks from my grandfather. Why should I pay you a fee for that?

"Mr. Jones, we do not believe in switching stocks either, neither do our managers. Many of our managers own stocks that were held from the initial public offering and are still rising in value. Stocks like Federal Express and Home Depot have been great investments from the day they were purchased, but circumstances change. Every good company has a problem. Coca-Cola is a superior company, right? So is Phillip Morris and IBM. These are successful companies with tremendous histories, but each has suffered corrections in a short period of time, greater than 50%, and that type of loss is not quickly recovered.

It is necessary to have professionals monitor your portfolio so that when companies do change adjustments can be made. Yes, we believe there are long-term holds when a company sustains fundamental value over time, but there are also times when great companies, like Coca-Cola, Phillip Morris, and IBM, go through periods of difficulty in their business practices. The competition becomes cosiderable and they need to be removed from the portfolio to eliminate their negative effect on the portfolio.

In many cases a person holds a single stock position that accounts for a substantially higher percentage of the total portfolio than it should. That position should be reduced because no matter how good the company is even great companies may go through difficult times. If you have an investment you strongly feel is a long-term hold we can separate it from your portfolio as necessary, but we do believe it is important to keep all good stocks under management so that when fundamentals change they can be moved."

You only have 40 managers in your program. How do I know these are the best?

"Mr. Jones, there is no such thing as the "best managers". We look for the most consistent managers in terms of business practices, the tenure of the management team, business philosophy, style of management, the process by which they manage their portfolio, and expenses. We do not look for the best. We look for the manager who most consistently satisfies their purpose in a portfolio. We hire managers who consistently manages money within their style, whether large growth, large value, small growth, etc. Performance is not made by the manager, it is made by a proper, prudent asset mix within the guidelines of the client risk profile."

EXPONENTIAL CHANGE

Sustainable Growth

A change starts with a vision of something different and leads to focused actions.

Ten Month Planning

Everyone plans for the future in some way whether formally with specific documented goals or informally, simply thinking along the lines of "I would like to do this," and, "I would like to do that." Whatever the method, we tend to plan for a year. One of the secrets of exponential change is focusing on 10 months rather than 12.

Benjamin Graham, in his books *Security Analysis* and *The Intelligent Investor*, discusses the necessity of having a margin of safety in your investment portfolio, a buffer zone that allows you, in the midst of a crisis or chaos, to have a safety net to protect you. When we plan for 12 months we leave ourselves no safety net. I believe a better strategy is to identify the 2 months during which you would like downtime. By focusing on achieving your plans in 10 months rather than 12 you give yourself a 20% margin of safety.

The months I recommend for downtime are December and the summer month during which you have the most difficult time contacting clients because they are on vacation. I believe December is not a month in which we should do business anyway. In most cases clients are centered on family and the social side of their lives, not business. Anyone you call in the month of December knows one thing; you are calling because you have to.

Once you decide on the months you have extra time in case of a crisis or disruption to your schedule to finalize your intended plans for the year. You can use two months to add the value needed to complete and exceed your goals for the year. Not using 10 month planning means you have no margin of safety and run the risk of underperforming if a disruption occurs. For example, if the market pulls back you have the opportunity to retrench, postpone vacation time, apply extra effort as necessary, and still meet and possibly exceed your expectations.

Consider running the business with a smaller staff during downtime so your team is given recreation time. Ten-Month Planning adds value to the lives of your team members who, in turn, create value in the lives of your clients.

This is your planning time. Take an afternoon off, focus on three years from now, and examine what changes you want to see in your practice. What do you want your life and your business to look like? What are the end results you want to see? Then have the team help you concentrate on the next 90-day period. Break it down week by week and focus on the actions and tasks that will help you accomplish your 3 year vision. These are your N.O.W. Tasks and there is No Other Way you can reach that vision unless you commit to these items. This exercise can create exponential change in your practice, whereby you meet or exceed the expectations you have for your team and for your business. It starts with 10 month planning and allowing yourself that extra margin of safety.

Ten Month Planning Process™

#1 - Think in 10 month time frame
#2 - Examine your legacy
#3 - Envision your five biggest changes
#4 - Meet with team and share benefits
#5 - Team identifies 90 Day Action Plan
#6 - Weekly team meetings

Four Steps to Implement Exponential Change

It is more important to have a greater understanding of how to implement change than it is to understand goal setting. Setting goals, for many, is a natural process. You set goals over and over and, as you set them, you achieve them then move to the next step and the next set of goals. Throughout the process you experience change, but what I endorse is not gradual change over time, but exponential change. Consider change in the form of radically transforming businesses and radically achieving stretch goals in substantially shorter periods with substantially less effort. I will take you through the Four Steps to Implement Exponential Change in an investment consulting practice. The exponential change concept unites vision, business planning, goal setting, and weekly actions, culminating all into one simple process.

The concepts teach you to concentrate efforts over four distinct time periods. The first is most broad. It covers your lifetime and the legacy you want to leave behind. The second period narrows to the next three years and is more easily visualized. Thirdly, you take account of the next 90 days or calendar quarter. Like seasons, 90-day time periods divide activity into distinct segments. Finally, you focus on the immediate week.

Lifetime Legacy

One overriding goal in everyone's life is to "Finish Well" - to finish well as an individual, to finish well financially, to finish well relationship wise, to finish well as far as the legacy you leave behind. Therefore, you must, as Stephen Covey says, "Begin with the end in mind." The ultimate goal is to Finish Well and realize, through a plan of action, which implements change in your life and make finishing well a reality.

The first step focuses on the legacy you want to leave behind and how you define Finishing Well. In Stephen Covey's book, *The Seven Habits of Highly Effective People*, he states that the easiest way to identify what you want to accomplish in life is to place yourself mentally at your wake and have the individuals you respect or the stakeholders in your life step up to your coffin and whisper what they think of your life. You may like some of what you hear, but not all of what you hear - both are beneficial.

Every major change I have made throughout my career and life comes about by going through an exercise like this and realizing the responses I hear are different than the results I seek. My initial decision to enter the financial services industry and my decision in the mid-1980s to move to managed money were decisions derived through such an exercise. The decision to create the Finish Well Network and focus on speaking, training, and coaching top financial service professionals came about as a result of one of these sessions. My later decision to retire from my practice and devote time to coaching and speaking again transpired because of this process. Each of these major changes in my life happened simply because I looked to the future and realized the result I wanted for my legacy was different than the track I established to that point.

For example, I applied this exercise in December of 1994. As every stakeholder in my life passed before my coffin, I felt comfortable with the responses from each one until I heard from my industry. I heard from my spouse, family, friends, neighbors, employees, and clients and was pleased with their comments, but when I reached the people from my industry, all they could say was, "Lloyd was a good consultant." I wanted to hear, "Lloyd made a difference in the industry," but to obtain that result I had to make a radical transformation in my career. I created the Finish Well Network and started focusing on my new lifetime legacy goal of training 10,000 advisors to transition their businesses to fees and add life to their lifestyles. That necessitated a major change in my business and was responsible for subsequent changes to my goals and actions.

As you apply this exercise, you may see a gap between where you are and where you want to be. The process of change bridges the gulf. To reiterate, the first step is to identify your lifetime legacy goals for the legacy you want to leave behind, the results you want by the end of your lifetime. Establish five legacy goals and focus your passion and motivation.

Three Year Vision

Established legacy goals impact what you want your life to look like in the next three years, the time frame for step two and the Three Year Vision Goals.

Consider the coming three years and what you want. This vision goal does not require the involvement of your team members. Think about how you want your business to look, who you want your clients to be, and where you want to take your business practice in the next three years. The answers to these questions establish, for you and the team, the direction for the business. List five major changes or results you desire which are different from where you are today. Label these Three Year Vision Goals.

90 Day Team Action Goals

After you establish the vision for the business and articulate five Three Year Vision Goals, communicate your conclusions to your team. Start the session by explaining the lifetime legacy you would like to leave and the three year vision you have for the business. Turn the meeting over to the team and ask them to identify the 10 most important steps to take in the next 90 days to move closer to accomplishing the vision goals. The 90 Day Team Goals will then be the focus and direction for the team over the next 13 weeks.

During this stage it is important that you, the consultant, talk little and allow the team to carry most of the discussion. It is also important early on to allow them to establish the goals for the next 90 days even if you disagree or believe the goals are too limited or shortsighted. Team members will establish a goal based on their comfort level as a group, which may be below your own comfort level. Realize that you are aiming for team buy-in. Too often, an advisor identifies a stretch goal without the buy-in of team members. Although the team may achieve the goal by being forced into action, they will do so against their will rather than with motivation and passion. That is why achieving a 20% or less growth curve tends to be the norm rather than a growth of 40% to 60%, which is the exponential growth achievable if the team takes ownership of the process.

Assume you determine you want to produce "x" million dollars over the next 3 year production cycle and your target is $250,000 per quarter in fee-based business. The team rationalizes that since they did $200,000 per quarter last year, they will probably only be able to do $210,000 this year. You think that estimate is too low, but accept it. Use the numbers the team agrees upon; in their mind, that number is a stretch goal. You see in the next stage how the team focuses on weekly action goals and how, over a 13 week period, the team will not only achieve the goals established, but typically exceed them. You will find that by accepting a lesser goal now, which has team buy-in, you will end up with superior results three years down the road, an outcome of exponential compounding change achieved when the whole team takes ownership of the growth of the business.

It is imperative to progress from the 90 Day Team Goals to the next stage, Weekly Action Goals. Failing to advance to Weekly Action Goals is the central reason for failure in goal setting. Many teams never break down the business plan into action items.

Weekly Action or N.O.W. Tasks

If you do not move 90 Day Team Goals into immediate action items you will have problems achieving exponential change. These are your Weekly Action Goals or what I call the N.O.W. list. There is No Other Way (N.O.W.) to achieve your 90 Day Team Goals without executing weekly actions. What action must be taken now toward the achievement of your Team Goals?

During your team meeting each week allocate 15 minutes to review the 90 Day Team Action Goals established by the team. These are the 10 items the group will focus on for the next thirteen weeks. The advisor's purpose during the 15 minute period is to establish 5 to 10 action or N.O.W. goals for the week, which bring you closer to achieving the 90 day goal.

Action items should be written down and assigned to individuals on the team. Through this process each team member has the opportunity to focus during the week on a specific action or task that brings the whole team closer to a desired result. The week's success or failure is measured according to how many of the N.O.W. goals are accomplished, identified by the percentage of accomplishment for the week.

If 100% of N.O.W. goals within the week are achieved, you had an extraordinary week and should celebrate with the team. Reward the accomplishment by treating the team to pizza or another perk. If you achieve 9 of 10 items, or 90%, you get an "A" for the week; 80%, a "B"; 70%, a "C". If you achieve 60% or less of the N.O.W. goals, that is an "F" and you flunked for the week. No matter what else happened during the week, the important things did not get done. You are trying to establish a habit of focusing on a 13 week action plan, a team habit of accomplishing and excelling at focusing on these team goals. Therefore, if you accomplish all 10 N.O.W. goals for the week, but did not raise new money, it was still a successful week. On the other hand, if you brought in a $1,000,000 new account, but accomplished only one N.O.W. goal, it was still a failure for the week. Three years from now that $1,000,000 account will have had an insubstantial impact on your goals in life. Creating the habit of achieving and excelling in your N.O.W. goals each week is the key to exponential growth.

During the last week of each quarter the team establishes a new set of 90 day goals that advance the Vision Goals. Every week the team re-establishes the most important N.O.W. activities necessary to achieve the goals and delegates the tasks among the team. Each team member should contribute to the N.O.W. goals for the week.

Every 90 days, prior to meeting with your team, re-establish and reconfirm the Lifetime Legacy Goals you want to achieve. Make certain your Three Year Vision is still valid because it does change over your lifetime.

Establish five Lifetime Legacy Goals and the Three

Year Vision Goals you have for your business. Set aside 30 minutes to an hour and meet with your team to explain your lifetime and Vision Goals. Establish the 90 Day Team Action Goals. Do not leave the meeting until you specify next week's N.O.W. list and every team member is assigned at least one task. At the end of the week, measure the achievement of the N.O.W. goals and celebrate success. By repeating this process over time, the team builds the discipline of overachieving which pays back to them in the growth of the business. It is important to move legacy and Vision Goals from your head to the hearts of the team members as they establish team goals and then to their feet as they step into the weekly N.O.W. list. The focus is concentrated from lifetime to a 3 year vision, to 90 day goals, then to a specific 7 day period. The application of focus, passion, energy, and time drives exponential growth.

Vision

The Prerequisite to Building a Better Team

Before we can discuss how to build a team, we must focus on the requirement that must precede all other thoughts or actions: vision.

Vision must come from the top down. Lee Iacocca did not leave the vision for Chrysler to the employees on the assembly line. He passionately stated, "This is our vision." Everyone accepted the vision and transformed Chrysler into a better business. Without a vision a team works without direction and motivation. While vision comes from the top down, implementation of that vision comes from the bottom up. It is the responsibility of each advisor to state the vision for his or her team.

The American Heritage Dictionary of the English Language* defines vision as:

vi-sion (v_zh_n) noun
1. a. The faculty of sight; eyesight: poor vision.
    b. Something that is or has been seen.
2. Unusual competence in discernment or perception; intelligent foresight: *a leader of vision*.
3. The manner in which one sees or conceives of something.
4. A mental image produced by the imagination.
5. The mystical experience of seeing as if with the eyes the supernatural or a supernatural being.
6. A person or thing of extraordinary beauty.

The important definitions for us are 1a, 3, and 4. Each focuses on the fact that a vision identifies something that does not necessarily exist at present. As Charles Allen once said, "What the mind of man can conceive and believe, it can achieve." This conception is the basis of the power of a vision. Stating your vision with passion makes it a reality to your team. The accomplishment of the vision is left to the team to implement.

Before discussing implementation, how do you go about creating a vision? First, schedule a weekend to get away for some private time. You will need at least four uninterrupted hours alone. Use that designated time to ask yourself two questions: What will my industry be like in five years? Contemplate the future. If you do not occasionally ask yourself this question, the future is likely to catch you unprepared. Write down all the things you think will change over the next five years.

Then ask yourself, what can I do today to prepare for the coming changes in my industry? Focus on the practical aspects of your business. What needs to happen to prepare you and your business for the changes you foresee? By answering this question and accounting for the conclusions, you will never be overwhelmed by the future. Take as much time as necessary to answer the two questions since they will assist you the rest of the day.

You have the raw material needed to create your vision. Envision what you want yourself and your business to look like in three years. Project and focus your thoughts to the future. Who are your clients? What are you doing? What has changed in your team? What technology do you have? What education or skills have you gained? Where do you live and work? When do you work? What do you do with your free time? What does a typical day look like? Continue asking yourself questions and envisioning what you and your business will look like.

When you have a clear picture, write it down. Begin with bullet points and list the business and lifestyle components of your future. Continue restating your future in clearer terms until you can explain it in less than a minute. You now have a vision for yourself and your business. Memorize your vision. Repeat it often.

Building a team is a journey and the first step is establishing your vision. People want to follow a leader with a clear vision who passionately believes in that vision.

ACTION PLAN

Transition to Fees Without Losing Revenue

The transition to fees process enables you to move your existing business to fee-based business in a simple systematic manner. Thousands of advisors have followed the steps to gradually build fee-based managed money practices.

Transitioning Process

1 - Homework

Household	Assets	
Robert Rollins	$ 1,500,000	Top 20%
Abe Abernathy	$ 1,200,000	
Johnny Jacobs	$ 1,000,000	
Beth Baker	$ -	
Doug Daniels	$ -	
Wallace Willis	$ -	
Vivian Vick	$ 750,000	
Thomas Tribble	$ 650,000	
Carl Christopher	$ -	Middle 60%
Eugene Ewing	$ -	
Molly McDonald	$ -	
Sampson Stevenson	$ -	
Frank Foster	$ -	
Kristi Klingman	$ -	
Hugh Harrison	$ -	
Greg Garrison	$ -	
Nick Nichols	$ -	
Laurie Lightner	$ 50,000	
Zack Zimmerman	$ 45,000	Bottom 20%
Quinn Queen	$ 42,000	
Paul Parsons	$ -	
Oscar O'Shay	$ -	
Yolanda Young	$ -	

List all households in declining asset order and draw a line under the Top 20% of households. Then draw another line under the first household with $50,000 ($100,000 if your revenue is $1,000,000 or more a year). Label the Middle 60%. You will find that the Top 20% control on average 73% of assets and revenue, the Middle 60% control 25%, and the Bottom 20% control less than 2%.

2 - Create Models

ALLOCATION MODELS

Category 5		
Asset Class	**% Allocation**	**Manager**
International-Developed	5%	ABC International
International – Emerging	15%	XYZ Emerging Markets
Large Growth Stocks	27.5%	ABC Growth
Large Value Stocks	27.5%	XYZ Value
Small Company Growth	10%	ABC Small Growth
Small Company Value	10%	XYZ Small Value
Bonds	0%	ABC Bond
Managed Futures	5%	XYZ Managed Futures

Category 4		
Asset Class	**% Allocation**	**Manager**
International-Developed	10%	ABC International
International – Emerging	4%	XYZ Emerging Markets
Large Growth Stocks	30%	ABC Growth
Large Value Stocks	30%	XYZ Value
Small Company Growth	6%	ABC Small Growth
Small Company Value	6%	XYZ Small Value
Bonds	10%	ABC Bond
Managed Futures	4%	XYZ Managed Futures

Category 3		
Asset Class	**% Allocation**	**Manager**
International-Developed	8%	ABC International
International – Emerging	3%	XYZ Emerging Markets
Large Growth Stocks	27%	ABC Growth
Large Value Stocks	27%	XYZ Value
Small Company Growth	5%	ABC Small Growth
Small Company Value	5%	XYZ Small Value
Bonds	21%	ABC Bond
Managed Futures	4%	XYZ Managed Futures

Category 2		
Asset Class	**% Allocation**	**Manager**
International-Developed	5%	ABC International
International – Emerging	0%	XYZ Emerging Markets
Large Growth Stocks	23%	ABC Growth
Large Value Stocks	23%	XYZ Value
Small Company Growth	0%	ABC Small Growth
Small Company Value	5%	XYZ Small Value
Bonds	40%	ABC Bond
Managed Futures	4%	XYZ Managed Futures

Category 1		
Asset Class	**% Allocation**	**Manager**
International-Developed	5%	ABC International
International – Emerging	0%	XYZ Emerging Markets
Large Growth Stocks	13%	ABC Growth
Large Value Stocks	13%	XYZ Value
Small Company Growth	0%	ABC Small Growth
Small Company Value	5%	XYZ Small Value
Bonds	60%	ABC Bond
Managed Futures	4%	XYZ Managed Futures

Create 5 or more risk models. Use numbers, not words, to identify the different risk models.

3 - Relationship Conversation With Each Household

Begin with the last name at the bottom of the Middle 60

and practice up the list. The conversation will establish a higher level of trust in the relationship. Schedule the transition call at the end of this conversation. Two weeks later followed up with a transition to fees call.

4 - Identify ROA and Print Holding

Avoid the high ROA accounts until you have worked through your entire list, then go back and transition those clients also.

5 - Input Data in Asset Allocation Software

Whether you use Allocation Master or your firm's optimization software, a team member inputs the client account data to determine the appropriate risk category.

6 - Print Asset Allocation Analysis

Print the asset allocation analysis in color and bind professionally for the Top 25 households.

7 - Create Proposal

1. Asset Allocation Analysis
2. Information describing investment choices
3. Paperwork necessary to open investment account
4. Return envelope

8 - Assistant Calls to Set Appointment

An assistant calls the client to schedule an appointment for the next week using the following script:

"Mr. Jones, the Investment Consulting Group purchased institutional software that enables us to conduct asset allocation analysis for our individual client accounts. In the past this software was only available to multi-million dollar, institutional clients. We would like to send the analysis to you and review it with you next week. May we schedule that appointment? "

9 - Advisor Makes Presentation

Continue to practice from the bottom of the Middle 60%, ascending your household list until you can answer "yes" to both questions below:

Do I know the presentation completely?
Can the team execute the paperwork flawlessly?

The Middle 60% presentations and transitions can be conducted over the telephone, if you have worked with them that way in the past, otherwise meet in person. The Top 20% appointments should be face-to-face meetings.

10 - Paperwork Processed

The team processes the paperwork and schedules the first review meeting.

Two Track Focus

While transitioning to fee-based managed money you must maintain a two track focus: transactional business and fee business. If you do not continue transactional business with non-fee clients your total revenue will decline substantially.

By opening all new business under a fee-based model and converting your book one client at a time you can have an established fee-based practice in a little over a year.

Advisor Model Day

8:00 - 12:00	Transactional Business
12:00 - 1:00	Lunch or Workout
1:00 - 3:00	Transition to Fees
3:00 - 5:00	Relationship Conversation

Important Note

If you will conduct one relationship conversation and one transition to fee presentation a day, four days a week. You can transition your top 200 clients in the first year and the rest of your clients the next year. At the end of the first year you will have a substantially enhanced business and life.

MANAGING YOUR TEAM

Your Greatest Resource is the Team that Supports Your Vision

One of the major reasons businesses plateau is the loss of information that occurs every time a team member is absent or leaves. Every team member is a brain trust of knowledge that the business has paid to create and store. The problem is only a few businesses have the means to maintain this storehouse of information.

The Necessity of Team Creativity

Introduction

The creation and development of an exponential business starts with your greatest resource: your team. You have passion, skill, and desire, but without a team to help deliver to the marketplace, you may struggle with constant obstacles. A motivated team that buys into your vision for the future can create exponential results and an outstanding impact on your life and the lives of clients.

Too often, an organization plateaus after experiencing success. The lull is usually attributable to an unmotivated team that does not buy into the vision laid out before them. Team buy-in is thwarted by lack of leadership, broken promises, lack of clarity or misunderstanding, or no involvement in the creation of the vision. Each shortfall creates a lack of motivation, a floundering business, inadequate client service, and loss of revenue and clients. Negative results can be avoided by understanding the dynamics that make a team successful, how to communicate with each other, the skills of each team member, and how to best utilize each member's skills to achieve the team's goals and objectives.

Exponential Team

What is an Exponential Team? An Exponential Team is defined as a group of individuals working toward a common vision who are knowledgeable, motivated, happy, healthy, and running the business on autopilot.

The team's results far outweigh the energy exerted because there is no wasted motion. Procedures exist for all operational tasks and eliminate wasted energy and effort. Clients's needs are understood and creative, innovative solutions are developed to solve client problems. A proactive service program is in place to anticipate needs and exceed client expectations, which leads to unlimited referrals.

An Exponential Team may seem an implausible force, but it is not. An Exponential Team does require what most teams do not have, the time and energy to cultivate, because they are overwhelmed with day to day activities of normal business. The solution is simple and effective, but requires a safe environment to encourage human beings to do what they are most gifted to do: create.

Creativity

Creativity is the ability or power to create. Human beings are creative animals. We are productive, creative beings characterized by originality and expressiveness. We are imaginative. We bring new things into existence through our imaginative skill. Think of obstacles that faced society throughout the ages and recall innovative solutions applied to disease, transportation, communication, exploration, science, and innumerable areas of life.

Team Creativity

How does creativity apply to our teams and why is it the starting place for establishing an Exponential Business? First, remember that communication is our most effective tool in a small team, and our most neglected skill. We forget that everyone communicates differently because we are all wired differently. Some communicate in long, detailed paragraphs while others talk in bullet points, condensing a discussion down to essential ingredients. Some like and understand numbers and others prefer to see and illustrate with pictures. These differences create communication gaps that lead to misunderstanding, confusion, and sometimes distress.

Given differences in communication styles, we need to create a safe place for open discussion, where each team member has the chance to give input. A freeform discussion is called brainstorming and is only possible if all participants feel free to say whatever comes to mind. We often self-edit ourselves in an open forum to avoid saying something that, after reflection, is "half-baked". Self-editing is the death of brainstorming because one person's "half-baked" idea might be the spark for another to bring forth a stellar idea.

By encouraging all members of the team to give input, ownership of the vision and team actions are accepted by all members, not just the leader. Once a team member realizes their input is desired and needed, a change occurs. Not only do they take ownership of the results, they are motivated and look for ways to become more involved. As a result, the team delivers proactive service on behalf of the client, solves the problem at hand, and anticipates subsequent needs. Team members act as a unit, in concert, for the benefit of clients, not just to meet expectations but proactively exceed expectations. Creativity is the catalyst behind such desired changes.

Conclusion

Before we can create exponential teams we must allow for open, honest communication among all team members. Encouraging creative thoughts and ideas produces innovative solutions for the team's problems first then clients's needs. Involvement is the fuel that moves the team forward. Creativity starts the engine that leads to change.

Resources:

The following books are useful resources to help you further understand the importance of creativity and how to develop creativity:

The Path of Least Resistance - Robert Fritz
How to Think Like Leonardo da Vinci - Michael Gelb
Drawing on the Right Side of the Brain - Betty Edwards

Criteria for Building a Team

Building a team requires careful thought, sound judgment, and important decisions. Circumstances often force rash decisions because we have no established standards or criteria for who we want to hire.

The team members you work with are important elements in your life. You spend more waking hours in a year with your team than with your own children or spouse. For this reason, your team is your business family. You do not allow just anyone into your family or home and neither should you allow just anyone to move into your business home.

When it comes to building and managing your team, do you sometimes feel behind the eight ball? This is a common concern for team leaders and requires understanding the criteria for team building.

By establishing simple criteria for team membership you ensure a happy, well motivated, and effective team. The suggested criteria are applicable to any business or industry.

Skill Set Needed

Team members do not need to know how to do a particular task, but must possess the personality, behavior, and communication skills that match what you require regarding a particular position. Then assess each team member using a standard testing tool like DISC or Myers-Briggs. These resources quickly inform you about a potential team member's aptitude for a role. Look for the raw material you can shape rather than someone fixed in their ways and unwilling to grow.

Willingness To Learn

Every business constantly evolves. Technology changes. Team members need to be open to new concepts and ideas. Look for people desiring a career rather than merely a job. Commit to a safe creative environment that encourages learning, and support each team member's efforts.

Future Focus

Every business aims to grow and take advantage of future opportunities. Team members must use the past as a springboard into the future. Avoid past-based individuals. Look for team members who have goals and aspiration to make those goals a reality.

These simple criteria assess a person from three perspectives: past, present, and future. They are the building blocks for establishing your own unique criteria for team membership. If you would like help in establishing your criteria or assessing a potential team member email office@lloydwilliamsinc.com.

Service: A Two-Part Job

For decades countless businesses believed they could function with one person handling all service related issues. This belief has become the great myth of small businesses.

Client service involves two separate skill sets. The first involves relationship development: answering the phone, scheduling appointments, meeting and greeting clients, representing the face of the team, ensuring necessary tools and materials are ready for the partners or consultant, and overseeing the front end of the organization. These team members like distraction and change, are sociable, and enjoy conversing and working with clients.

The second skill set entails process management: handling paperwork, attending to details, organizing information, possessing extraordinary follow through habits, provide technology support, and being task-minded and process-oriented. These team members like systematic procedures and prefer working with paper instead of people. They are meticulous and have superior follow through skills. They prefer the operational side of business.

Achieving Team Buy-In

Achieving team buy-in is simple if team members consider your vision worthy, see a direct benefit to themselves and the client, and have an active role in the achievement of the vision. If you meet these three specifications, team buy-in happens naturally.

The reasons team buy-in may not be achieved are as follows:

Broken Promises

You will not gain team buy-in from a team member who feels promises were made to him or her, but not kept. A breach in the contract was effected, so to speak, and the person lost trust.

Wrong Position, Wrong Industry

A team member in the wrong position or wrong industry

will not likely buy into the future of your team. Individuals mismatched for their position will not buy into something they do not see themselves a part of or wanting to be a part of in the future.

Past Experiences and Perceptions

Sometimes a team member, who in the past worked for someone of lower integrity, may view the industry as corrupt and has no trust for the profession in general.

No Leadership

Team members will not buy into your vision if they see lack of leadership. Perhaps ideas are set in motion, but they flounder without leadership.

Foreign Experiences

You may ask a team member to do something that is foreign to their life experience. Perhaps they have never had to set goals. They have never experienced achieving an established goal. You ask them to do things outside their normal experience. Such team members can buy into your vision, but they need to get through the learning curve first.

To help your team avoid these five problems focus on a worthy vision that benefits team members and clients and let each team member participate in the execution of that vision.

Criteria for Team Infrastructure

An exponential team is defined as a group of individuals working toward a common vision, who are knowledgeable, motivated, happy, healthy, and running a business on autopilot.

Expertise

Partners and consultants are the reasons clients come in the first place. Partners and consultants are responsible for helping the client to think strategically about their life and future. A team provides service that solves client problems, therefore, team members must be knowledgeable in the field.

Communication

A client's first impression lasts and necessitates a favorable reception by the team. The communications team member meets, greets, and functions as concierge for the client. They act as the face of the organization. All scheduling, calls, and meetings are organized and directed by them. A communications team member serves as flight control for the team, handling short-term client issues and guiding the new client into the team. This is a required position no matter how small the team.

Operations

Attention to details rewards a team in numerous ways. The operations team member must be a process person with great follow through skills. They maintain the top-notch service that high net worth clients expect. This team member has the opportunity to cement the client relationship by exceeding expectation, by being proactive in problem solving. This is a required position no matter how small the team.

Relationship

Advocacy is built because of the little things. The relationship manager maintains the relationship and deepens the team's involvement in managing the client's life. This team member keeps the focus on the client's needs and on creating innovative solutions to client problems. Partners or consultants can handle this position until the team grows.

Technology

Systems and procedures must run smoothly and they depend on having correct and accessible information. The technology team member is responsible for all deliverables to the client and ensuring information is available when needed. The communication member can handle this position until the team grows.

While building your team remember the importance of hiring prudently in the first place. The cost and loss of time as a result of retraining team members is extremely unproductive.

Cost of Not Hiring

Many business leaders believe the cost of hiring is too high for results received.

When we consider the true cost of employment, we often forget to include the increase in productivity of team members in the calculation. To illustrate, imagine a team with no assistants. The advisor must do everything. Their productivity suffers. Often a full-time employee is viewed as a luxury that costs too much. Not true.

First, entrepreneurs do not have business expenses, they make business investments that have a positive return or they stop the investment, whether a factory, a machine, or the greatest resource, an employee. A business expense is an accounting concept created for the tax man. As business owners, we make investments in our business to leverage our skills and strengths.

Second, we must understand our Money Making Hourly Rate™. This is the hourly amount we are worth to the business during money making activities. To calculate, account for the following: (1) total assets raised last year, (2) multiply by ROA for gross revenue generated, (3) number of households involved, (4) time spent making closing presentations to raise the assets, and (5) divide the hours into gross revenue. The result is your Money Making Hourly Rate™.

Example:

Step 1	Total Assets Raised	$10,000,000
Step 2	Gross generated	1% ROA = $100,000
Step 3	Households	20
Step 4	Time in Presentations	2 hours each = 40
Step 5	Divide Hours in Gross	$2500
	Money Making Hourly Rate™	**$2500 per hour**

Suppose a team decides to hire an assistant to handle administrative and operational tasks which are not primary skills of the business owner who is best skilled at relationship building and strategic thinking and that the assistant is only one fourth as good at the tasks as the owner. Suppose an assistant with the necessary skill set is hired, paid $3,000 a month, and works forty hours per week. Assume they eliminate at least 25% of the tasks the owner undertook originally, freeing up ten hours per week for the owner to focus on money making activities that, earlier, were unable to be dealt with given the operational tasks occupying the owner's time. Ten hours a week adds forty hours a month to money making activity.

Utilizing the additional forty hours of money making activity time would more than cover the assistant's $3,000 monthly salary. The excess is extra profit.

To find the cost of not hiring the assistant multiply the Money Making Hourly Rate™ by 40 and subtract $3,000. That is the monthly cost of not having an assistant.

The Hiring Process

The hiring process is a method of engaging the services of another for a specific role within in an organization.

Hiring an individual involves a significant investment in a business. Make certain the right person is hired the first tim and reduce the risk of costly turnover. Be confident the new hire will add value to existing skills and strengths of the team and promote greater productivity. The only way to secure these results is to have a method easily executed and repeated. Build a team with the following 10 Step Hiring Process.

1 - Define

Define the job and skill set required. First, define what needs to be accomplished. This can be a job description or list of tasks to assign. Too often this initial step is overlooked. A person should be hired for a specific role with well defined objectives which enables the applicant to exemplify their skill set and the company to determine a suitable match.

2 - Advertise

Advertise for applicants selectively. Do not place an ad in the paper. Focus your search to specific groups of applicants.

Operations applicants can be sought through referrals from clients since they are most difficult to find in the job marketplace. Communications applicants may be found through temp agencies, people you meet in the retail marketplace, servers, receptionists, and sales people.

3 - Screen

Screen, conduct an initial interview, and skill test applicants. Create a simple skills test for related tasks and test each applicant. The initial interview concerns skill sets and whether the applicant meets the minimum required skill level or not. Look for a good base level of skill to build upon.

4 - DISC

Each team member should have a DISC assessment to

explicate how they prefer to communicate and what motivates them. This tool is valuable in dealing with communication barriers in small teams. For more information email office@lloydwilliamsinc.com.

5 - Narrow

Narrow the selection to the best candidates. Select the most skilled and best suited for the team.

6 - Interview

Conduct a formal interview. Remember, you spend more time with the people you work with than your family. Make sure they are someone you want in your business family. Share the vision you have for the business and how their role fits into the whole.

7 - Trial

Determine a trial work period. Schedule a time for the applicant to work with the team on a trial basis, even if only for a day or two. This will help determine compatibility and may be completed during the applicant's vacation time or other days off from employment.

8 - Agreement

Use a contract and confidentiality and non-solicitation agreement. Non-competition agreements do not always hold up in court. Your team and business handle a tremendous amount of confidential information; this information is property of the business and is not to be used by competitors. When every team member signs a non-solicitation and confidentiality agreement, concerns about information leaking to competitors if an employee leaves is eliminated. All severance arrangements are negotiated and agreed upon up front.

9 - Review

Review the member's progress and establish benchmarks. Establish quarterly reviews and benchmarks to measure progress.

10 - Encourage

Encourage success and creativity. Create an environment that encourages creativity and promotes successful results.

Caution: beware of hiring from within your industry. Frequently the individual carries perceptions and beliefs from previous experiences that hinder their ability to buy into your vision and team. (See Achieving Team Buy-In)

Hiring the Right Person for the Job

Once you establish a Criteria for Building a Team outline and understand that service is a two-part job, make certain the right person is hired. Assessments are one of the greatest tools to assist in hiring. Almost all assessments stem from research conducted by Carl Jung and pertain to the four personality types. Many tools have been created to better understand the relationship between the different personalities. Myers-Briggs Type Analysis is the granddaddy of all assessments and is used extensively in clinical research. For the small team this tool is a bit overwhelming and difficult to interpret.

The DISC is a simpler tool. The letters in DISC represent the four basic personality traits: Dominance, Influence, Supportive, and Compliant. By using the DISC, a team can identify where their strengths lie and where gaps in team dynamics reside. The DISC helps a team understand communication and behavioral traits, what individuals value, and what motivates each team member. These are important factors to be aware of when working with and managing team members.

For these reasons, we recommend that every team member complete a DISC Assessment. A DISC assessment is made up of two parts, the DISC and the PIAV (Personal Interest, Attitudes, and Values assessment). Each assessment takes about 10 minutes to complete online and results are emailed in a PDF file immediately to the individual and the team coordinator.

Nine Ways to Say Thank You to Your Team

One of the greatest challenges we face as financial consultants is motivating our team members. The difficulty stems from the fact that different things motivate different individuals. Some people are motivated by utilitarian elements like money or tangible items whereas others are motivated by intangibles, a word of praise, time off, or a pat on the back. What motivates you is not necessarily the same as what motivates your team. Given such differences, it is important to understand what motivates each person on a team.

A Nine Ways to Say Thank You exercise quickly identifies each team member's motivators and provides the manager of the team appropriate ideas for thanking team members in certain circumstances.

First, ask each team member to identify 3 ways, which have no monetary cost involved, to thank them or let them know you appreciate him or her. An example is to say, "thank you," or extend praise in front of other team members. Ask each person to list 3 ways he or she would like to be shown appreciation in a manner that could be done quickly, in the moment, and without cost.

Next, ask them to list 3 ways you could show appreciation that would cost up to a predetermined figure, maybe $100 or $250. Choose the figure according to the size of your team and what you can budget. Examples of a tangible thank you might be dinner out with a spouse or significant other, a manicure, a half-day at the spa, or a case of a favorite wine. You may be very surprised by the list and find the team member chooses things very different from what you would select for yourself or for that person.

Lastly, for extraordinary times when major goals are accomplished, or a team member acts significantly above and beyond the call of duty, ask them to list 3 ways you can say thank you if there were an unlimited budget. Examples of ideas might be a trip to Cancun, a week's vacation in Europe to attend cooking school in Tuscany, or a shopping trip to New York City.

Keep a list of nine ways to say thank you to each team member. The first three items are for small tasks or something accomplished that is important to the team and needs a prompt show of appreciation or "thank you." Use the second list for 90 day or intermediate-term periods when something fairly important is accomplished for the team's benefit. This list provides a bigger way of saying thanks, which requires some investment, but shows emphatic appreciation. When milestones are reached, when 3 Year Visions become reality exponentially faster than expected due to efforts of one or more team members, you can say thank you in a big way. If you achieve your 3 Year Vision in 18 to 24 months, you can afford to generously reward a team member.

By completing this exercise, team members understand their contribution to the team is valuable to you and that you reward their efforts. This thanks may give team members a chance to do things they might not do on their own. Perhaps they would not want to spend the money required to take that dream vacation, but as a gift from you, it is possible.

The three levels of reward and thanks provide a way of showing appreciation that matches the accomplishment, whether small or large, an important task or a major milestone.

Worksheet

List three ways you would like to be shown appreciation, which have no monetary value attached. (For example, word of thanks, recognition within team)
1.
2.
3.

List three ways you would like to be shown appreciation that cost up to $_____.
1.
2.
3.

List three ways you would like to be shown appreciation if the budget was unlimited.

1.
2.
3.

Team Procedures

This section describes how to create and maintain your team's storehouse of knowledge.

One major reason businesses plateau is the loss of information that occurs every time a team member leaves or is temporarily absent. Every team member is a brain trust of knowledge the business paid to create and store. The problem is few businesses have the means to maintain this storehouse of information.

The Great Brain Drain

The brain trust of a business should stay with the business, not walk out the door when a team member leaves. Too often the only knowledge of how a task is accomplished is in the head of the person who performed the task for the business. That knowledge leaves with them if they move on to other opportunities. The business is forced to retrain a replacement, often without the help of the person with the knowledge, which suspends business growth. The longer the retraining process takes, the further behind the business falls.

The secret to a smooth running business is consistent, repeatable procedures and operations. The knowledge each team member has needs to be documented and maintained. Since the information is not already documented there is reluctance to promote a team member to a position with added responsibility for fear of losing the current capability. Holding back the team member stunts growth of a business and contributes to progressing only enough to hit another plateau.

First, businesses have step-by-step procedures used every day to accomplish tasks. These procedures make up a checklist of tasks to perform in a specific order to accomplish the given project. Because the procedures already exist, the task is almost completed. You must capture the steps and document them.

Documenting Procedures

The idea of writing a procedures manual is daunting, which prevents most teams from doing so. All knowledge changes and without the procedures written down the information will be lost or costly to reacquire. Individuals continually retool themselves and add new information to facts already known on a daily basis. It becomes a personal habit, a habit that should carry over to create a business habit.

Modern technology makes documenting anything simpler than just a few years ago. With a digital recorder a procedure can be spoken, transcribed, and documented in the same day. When my team originally created our Operations Manual it took us six months to complete the process. Today a sample exists that only requires your team to edit and revise.

Go to website http://lloydwilliamsinc.com/wp-content/uploads/Ops_Manual.doc to download the sample.

Cross-Training

A Business Mistake

Cross-training is a common business practice that can cause team problems. The corporate world is full of buzz words for techniques to solve business troubles, techniques that often create more problems than they fix. Cross-training is one of many widespread practices that has become such a buzz word. The concept is simple: two or more team members capable of performing a specific task and the business is always able to deliver. Cross-training seems an apt solution. Instead of training one person for a task, train two and when one is out for some reason the other is capable of carrying out the task.

The reality is different. Because two separate team members are responsible for a specific task, neither takes ownership. It can always be the other person's responsibility. Without responsibility and ownership team members lack buy-in.

A larger problem is the loss of productivity of both team members. Even when a task is assigned to a primary and secondary backup, the team suffers because the productivity of the secondary backup is interrupted when they are required to step in to fill the gap. The disruption seems insignificant at the time, but every distraction requires 15 minutes to re-engage a team member's focus and previous activity, which adds up over time. If the team member steps in for several days then a backlog of their primary function creates its own problem. The problem compounds when several team members are involved. The time and money meant to be saved is eaten up in the creation of several backlogs of secondary importance. A mountain of unfinished projects and tasks accumulate.

It is necessary to have access to a temporary employee who is able to step in and allow other team members to continue functioning normally. This might seem extravagant to some, but the lack of team downtime more than covers the cost, and continuation of the momentum the team created results in notable profitability.

Documentation is required to make an Operations Manual an actuality. The manual details the steps necessary to accomplish a task. These step by step instructions can be followed by a temporary team member. Even if the temporary member functions at 60-80% of the capacity of the usual employee, little or no backlog is created for other team members.

Creating an Operations Manual

The Simplest Tool for Eliminating a Business Plateau

Consultants spend most of their time in the marketing and consulting aspects of business, commonly forgetting the operational and service areas handled by other team members. Because a consultant cannot service all client needs with a solo practice, they rely on the services of other members of the organization. Although fully occupied with the aspects of finding and raising money or managing the process for clients, consultants must simultaneously put effort toward managing the business. Included in managing is the people and resources they work with as an organized team.

The skills that contribute to success as a consultant are not typically the skills that make a good team manager. Team building requires a different skill set.

With a desire to cover shortages in manpower, a team may be trained so everyone can do everybody else's jobs. In theory it may seem a prudent approach, in practice it leads to chaos at worst and lack of ownership of a role at best. See the section Cross-Training: A Business Mistake for further explanation.

For the team to function members must know the specific duties and responsibilities he or she has. Every person on the team has a specialty. That specialty is his or her role on the team. An organized team is made of certain people doing certain jobs. A disorganized team consists of each person performing several roles regardless of assignment. Each person functions in his or her own assigned role and is a specialist. An Operations Manual is a notebook or folder kept by the person defining and describing his or her role in the team. An Operations Manual can be defined as a job description, but is much more.

Operations Manual includes the following:

- The purpose of the position on the team
- A copy of the organizational chart, clearly showing his or her place in the organization
- A write-up of duties involved in the position
- A detailed checklist of all duties of the position
- A flow chart showing what items are received by that person, what changes he or she is expected to make, and where the items are routed
- A description of the member's primary product
- A way to measure the product against a benchmark

When all team members know exactly what is expected of each other jobs and projects are easily delegated. Everyone is measured by a statistic that relates directly to what he or she produces. The additional value of the manual is that the entire job is defined in writing. When a person is promoted or leaves the team, his or her replacement has a detailed write-up of the role's duties which reduces training time and cost.

To create an Operations Manual, start with the purpose of the position. The purpose of the role can be jointly agreed upon by conversing with each team member. Then duties and actions can be recorded in a checklist and again agreed upon. The process continues until the manual is complete. Each team member is able to take ownership of the defined role and its responsibilities. The team can be directed as a working whole, rather than dictating action by action. Each member takes responsibility and ownership of his or her part of the process and the consultant can focus attention where it best serves clients and the team. Team members are empowered and have the necessary tools necessary to accomplish the task set before them. Because the consultant jointly agreed with the team member on the details upfront, the team member is free to work within the boundaries set. Constant monitoring of each person is not required. The workplace becomes relaxed and efficient.

A sample Operations Manual is available online at http://lloydwilliamsinc.com/wp-content/uploads/ Ops_Manual.doc.

Important Note: Please page break each task before using.

A Team On Autopilot

Imagine what your business would be like if everything ran smoothly and efficiently without your input. Everyone dreams of the perfect workday. When everything is completed on time, we have a sense of accomplishment at the end of the day and the environment is happy and creative. That state is an attainable ideal, it just requires focus and effort to become a reality.

First, understand the necessity of supporting the strengths of the entrepreneur who leads the team. Next, create an environment that encourages creativity. Realize each team member brings a specific set of skills to the team that must be dedicated to specific tasks. Only then can the team begin to proactively solve client problems. Over time continuity and consistency develop into team habits that clients value for themselves and referrals.

Support Our Strengths

Every entrepreneur has a unique set of skills that compliments their passion. The purpose of the team is to support the entrepreneur's expertise and allow the entrepreneur to focus their time and effort on exercising their expertise. When the entrepreneur's time is spent on activities outside their expertise the entire team is held back. When the team fills gaps and permits the entrepreneur to stay focused on their expertise the entire organization moves forward with growth.

Environment That Encourages Creativity

A team functions on autopilot only when honest communication is encouraged and their participation compels creativity to flourish. By becoming involved in the process and having ownership of the outcome, the team drives the business forward because they have a vested interest. Team members are no longer employees, but involved associates. Team leaders can create and encourage an atmosphere of communication and involvement.

Maximize Team Skills

Each team member brings a unique set of skills and

strengths to the business. Forgetting weaknesses and focusing on the strengths of each team member enables the team to match skills to specific tasks. Each task is performed by the most capable team member, increasing efficiency and producing the best results. Expect excellence from your team. An organization rises to the level of expectation. This is one reason why hiring the right people is so important.

Proactively Solve Client Problems

By concentrating on a client's unmet needs the team on autopilot looks for the solution to the unasked question, anticipates the next concern, and proactively creates a solution. Proactivity sets the team apart from all other teams and creates a WOW experience for the client.

Continuity and Consistency

By systematizing procedures teams can deliver services in a consistent manner. Continuity establishes the means to building advocacy in a client base.

The Exponential Business Score

Measuring your team as an autopilot organization can benchmark your progress.

What is required to create an autopilot organization that meets and exceeds the expectations of your clients? By scoring the steps you discover where you are today and what areas need your focused effort to improve your practice for the future.

Test yourself on the following page.

My business includes:		Score
Score each 1-10 (1 = nonexistent & 10 = true 100% of the time)		
Step 1:	A team that supports my passion and strengths	
Step 2:	An infrastructure that encourages creativity	
Step 3:	A focus on the client, not the business	
Step 4:	A Relationship Conversation™ with all Top 100 clients and prospects	
Step 5:	Identify our client's greatest Unmet Need	
Step 6:	Create a specific, Creative Solution for each client	
Step 7:	Walk the client through all necessary analysis for clarity	
Step 8:	WOW our client with an Innovative Solution using in-house and outside resources	
Step 9:	Monitor the profitability of our operation to enhance our delivery	
Step 10:	A plan for Finishing Well in all areas of our team's life.	

Stop The Distractions

Communication Assistant's Script

Assistant:
"Hello, this is (Assistant). How may I assist you?"

Client:
"May I speak with (Consultant)?"

Assistant:
If you do not recognize the voice ask, "To whom am I speaking?"

Client:
"This is (Client)."

Assistant:
"Mr./Ms. (Client), (Consultant) is in a conference right now. Because you are a valued client, he/she will want to make sure you are taken care of immediately. If you will tell me the reason for your call, we will pull your file so (Consultant) can have all of your information in front of him/her when he/she returns your call."

Client:
"I would like to talk about _____."

Assistant:
If it is a service related question say, "Mr./Ms. (Client) you do not have to wait, that is not something (Consultant) can help you with. That is handled by me or (Service Assistant) and I/he/she can help you right now."

If it is a service related question and the Service Assistant is busy say, "Mr./Ms. (Client) you do not have to wait for

(Consultant). That is not something he/she can help you with. That is handled by (Service Assistant) and he/she is on the phone at present. We will pull your file so he/she can have all of your information in front of him/her when he/she returns your call. Will you be available for a call within the hour? What is the best number to call?

If it is a consultant question (make sure you understand the question) say, "We will pull your file so he/she can have your information in front of him/her when he/she returns your call this afternoon. Would (specific time) be a good time for him/her to call?" If not, set a specific telephone appointment for later that day or the next.

COUNTERINTUITIVE

Investing is Not Intuitive

The reason many investors struggle with investing relates to the myth that investing is just common sense. Investing is counterintuitive and many long held assumptions are false.

Important Terms

Asset Allocation is the only concept powerful enough to require a client to make a radical change in their portfolio.

Asset Allocation

The correlation of the risks of different asset classes.

Diversification

Spreading investments over several enterprises or products to reduce risk of loss.

Correlation*

S&P 500 1.00
Large Value 0.97
Large Growth 0.95
International 0.85

DIVERSIFICATION 0.55

Small Value 0.50
Small Growth 0.45
Bonds (Historically) 0.35
Emerging Countries 0.20
Managed Futures 0.15

(*These are average long-term correlations)

Risk

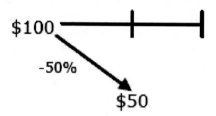

Losses have greater negative impact than profits have positive benefit.

A 50% loss requires a 100% gain to return to original investment. If you do not lose money you do not have to make much to still outperform.

An Example Worth Noting

In 1997 the market grew 26% in one year while experiencing 21% in downside volatility. Many investors created portfolios designed to outperform the market. Surprisingly, the ones that did outperform were designed to reduce risk and were expected to underperform.

Most portfolios are designed to outperform. They result in equal or higher beta with the market. As the market fluctuates the higher beta portfolios do outperform. In the up cycles the portfolio increases at a faster rate, resulting in greater short-term performance. When the market declines they also outperform. But in this case the losses are greater and because "losses have a greater negative impact than profits have a positive benefit", the end result, like 1997, is underperformance at the end of the year. They win some of the battles and lose the war.

A properly diversified and properly allocated portfolio underperforms in up cycles, but loses less money in down cycles and because it avoided the losses and participated in the rally the portfolio has a risk adjusted return for the period.

Counterintuitive Questions

Question #1

Where on the following chart would a 50% bonds and 50% stocks portfolio be plotted?

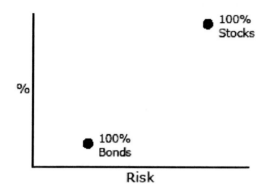

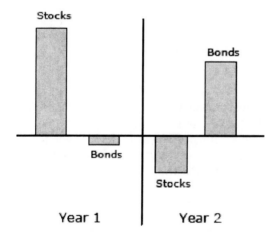

The intuitive answer is half way between the two dots. That is the wrong answer. The efficient frontier bends backwards and the 50/50 portfolio would be above the 100% bond dot with a higher rate of return because the difference in the correlation of stock to bonds. The average return of a rebalanced 50/50 portfolio over time substantially outperforms with almost the same risk.

Question #2

Where would the portfolio of the four equally weighted managers, indicated by the white circles below, be situated in the chart below?

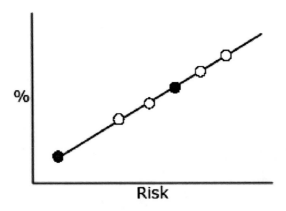

The intuitive answer is on the black index dot in the middle. That would be the wrong answer because the portfolio composite would move to the upper left. Diversification reduces risk and increases returns until diversified to the point of diminishing returns.

Question #3

What do you add to a portfolio to make it more conservative?

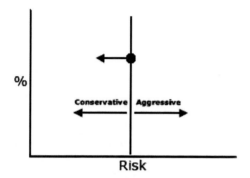

The intuitive answer is bonds, a conservative investment. That would be the wrong answer. Referring to the correlation table earlier in this chapter, you can see that either small-cap or managed futures with lower correlation to a balanced portfolio reduces overall risk and increases potential return.

This is a generic discussion and individual portfolios differ. The point is that the intuitive answer is often the wrong answer or less than the best answer.

Question #4

Which portfolio is best and why?

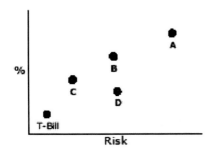

The intuitive answer is normally A or B - wrong answers. First, we need to ask ourselves what the risk and performance would be for a perfect investment. It would have no risk and unlimited performance. Though that is impossible that would be a perfect investment and a line pointing to its dot would be vertical from the T-bill. Therefore, the best investment would have a line closest to vertical. This is called Slope Analysis and is easy to do with a straight edge ruler. Line one edge of the ruler on the T-bill and set the ruler horizontal along the risk axis. Begin pivoting the ruler up until it connects with the D dot. This is the worst performing of the four portfolios on a risk adjusted basis. Continue pivoting up the page, A is next, followed by B and finally C. C is the best risk adjusted portfolio. If you draw lines starting at the T-bill and intersect each dot individually, you see the line for C is more vertical. For portfolio A or B to equal C on a risk adjusted basis they would have to reduce risk or increase return. You can draw a horizontal line to the left of each dot to represent the reduction in risk required as it crosses the C line or draw a vertical line up from the dot to represent the increase in performance.

Manager Selection

The Way Most Managers Are Selected

1 - Performance
2 - Price
3 - Process
4 - Philosophy
5 - People

The Correct Criteria for Manager Selection

1 - People
2 - Philosophy
3 - Process
4 - Price
_____
= Performance

Manager Interview Script

Each month you should contact every manager on a due diligence call to confirm that no changes have occurred within the firm and that the same people are doing the same thing the same way at the same price structure. The following script will help you begin your due diligence call to ensure accurate information from the manager:

"This is John Doe of ABC Securities, a member firm of the New York Stock Exchange. This is a recorded due diligence call."

Then ask questions to confirm that the same people are making the same decisions in the same way for the same costs.

PRESENTATIONS TO MOVE MONEY NOW

Client Education is the Secret

The following presentations are tools to help you educate your clients.

How to Move Stagnant Money Now

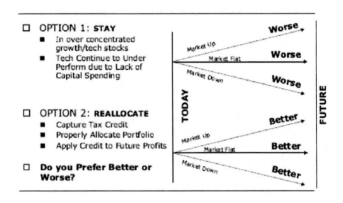

☐ OPTION 1: STAY
  ■ In over concentrated growth/tech stocks
  ■ Tech Continue to Under Perform due to Lack of Capital Spending

☐ OPTION 2: REALLOCATE
  ■ Capture Tax Credit
  ■ Properly Allocate Portfolio
  ■ Apply Credit to Future Profits

☐ **Do you Prefer Better or Worse?**

Event vs. Economic-Driven Corrections

What makes the stock market go up? What is a market rotation and what causes it to occur? What makes the stock market fall? These simple questions and resulting answers are often misunderstood. Cash is what makes the markets rise and fall. If you destroy either the creation of cash (deflation) or the purchasing power of cash (inflation) the market declines. The market declines two ways.

Event-Driven Correction

The correction begins following an event that shakes investor confidence and continues until rational minds realize the impact is insignificant to the economy and the market returns to where it was prior to the event. Event-driven corrections happen often.

Economic-Driven Correction

The correction is preceded by an eroding of the underlying economic base and the market declines until it adjusts for this reduced economic base. Economic-driven corrections rarely occur. Examples are: 1896-97, 1929-32, and 1973-74.

The S-Curve

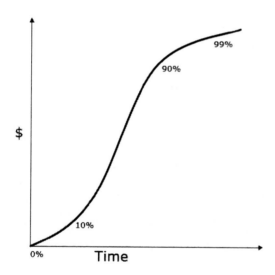

The S-Curve is used to analyze various aspects of a company or industry like market share, growth, market penetration, capacity, etc. When any industry or group reaches 10% market penetration there is an inevitable shakeout of the industry. Only the strong companies survive to climb the curve from 10% to 90%. This was illustrated clearly as the internet companies reached 10% market penetration as reported in Fast Company Magazine in 1999.

Ten Trends for the New Millennium

These trends are the cash cows that will drive the markets of the future.

Trend 1 - Baby Boomers Turn 50

The demographic impacts of the baby boom generation are well documented.

Trend 2 - Wealth Transfer

Baby boomers have parents that control almost $13 trillion dollars in the US and $2 trillion in Canada. These funds are held predominantly in cash (deposits) and real estate (family home), neither of which the child will hold. That is why banks buy brokerage firms. Baby boomers do not roll over CDs and the banks had to buy where their deposits were going. The investment of $15 trillion dollars into the markets will be pivotal.

Trend 3 - Global New Frontiers

From the 15th to 19th centuries world powers had to cross oceans and fight wars to take advantage of the new frontier of the Americas. Today the new frontiers are landlocked to the world powers. North America has the new frontier of Central and South America. Europe's new frontier is Eastern Europe and India. Japan and China's new frontier is China itself and southeast Asia. The opportunities for trade and joint economic growth are staggering.

Trend 4 - Corporate Retirement Plans

Retirement plans are growing at an extraordinary rate. Just the reinvestment of contributions and employer matching will be a stabilizing force in the markets.

Trend 5 - New Technology

Technology will continue to drive growth. Remember the internet is only just over 10% market penetration. What will the markets look like if it grows to 90%?

Trend 6 - Widening Distribution of Wealth

If you could go back in time you would find that wealth was predominantly controlled by one individual at a time - a king, a pharaoh, or an emperor - and these men or women tended to have ultimate power. The wealth they controlled was the leverage they had over the people beneath them. Move ahead to the 1890s, which was discussed in the Five Trends section, a time when 12 individuals amassed virtually all the wealth of the world. The incalculable wealth of an emperor in the past was then very tangible in a J. Paul Getty or John D. Rockefeller; a Morgan or a Mellon; a Gould, Bell, or Ford. These men were extremely wealthy.

Today, we have millionaires and billionaires, and we

create new millionaires and billionaires. The distribution of wealth is still broadening just not quite as deep. Billionaires today are not nearly as wealthy as those in the 1890s. John D. Rockefeller was 16 times wealthier than Bill Gates, yet John D. Rockefeller was insignificantly wealthy compared to the power and wealth of a pharaoh or a king. But Bill Gates is still wealthy, Paul Allen is still wealthy, and all of the individuals at the top of the business and economic food chain have significant wealth, but we are not talking about 12 people anymore, rather a widening number of individuals becoming wealthy. As the new frontier of development grows, we are closing the gap by raising the level of those in Third World nations. As they take on a capitalistic business model and become business owners themselves, the gap narrows as the distribution of wealth widens across the spectrum.

Trend 7 - Baby Boomer One-Stop Shopping

Baby boomers like convenience, fast food, and ease. The biggest phenomenon of the 80s and 90s was the superstore: Wal-Mart Superstore, K-Mart Superstore, Home Depot. These are companies that come into one location and service multiple areas. Where once a small town had a paint shop, a lumber store, a wallpaper store, a furniture store, and a hardware store, one Home Depot has replaced all of those businesses. The same thing has happened with Wal-Mart Superstores. Instead of having a grocery store, a convenience store, a pharmacy, and a five-and-dime, we now have a superstore that includes automotive items, electronics, and groceries all under one roof. As well, the mall has replaced the strip center and virtually destroyed the downtown areas of most small communities.

But the baby boomer likes one-stop shopping for services

and that is why the independent advisor out there needs to connect into a larger network of services. This is why Smith-Barney, Merrill Lynch, and Citibank combine services. A client can work with one consultant and have any financial service taken care of, whether a mortgage, mezzanine financing, stock options, investments, financial planning, or retirement planning. Whatever the client needs, all of it can be taken care of in one location. Build your business around a one-stop shop concept.

Trend 8 - Web-Based Delivery of Services

The Internet is pervasive and though there is 10-12% penetration now, it will become even more pervasive with time. It will have a deeper and deeper connection to the community and hearts and minds of consumers. For this reason, you need a web-based delivery system. Technology cannot turn intellectual property into a commodity in the market or on the Internet, but execution and delivery can be easily commoditized. That is the strength of the Internet and the weakness of the bricks-and-mortar model. As you evaluate your business and firms, begin as quickly as possible to learn and understand the web and grow in your ability to deliver your services quickly and efficiently over the web. One of the most powerful pieces of information you can gather from a client is their e-mail address and one of the most powerful educations you can give a client is how to access information on the web.

Trend 9 - The Virtual Office

Commuting is a terrible expense of both time and stress and costly in terms of dry cleaning, clothes, wear-and-tear on a car, and so on. As cities grow larger and larger, there is a necessity to tap into resources that might not be found locally. Technology today allows us to communicate over great distances instantaneously through instant messaging and at the same time we are able to work with others reviewing and editing documents through video conferencing, teleconferencing, and e-mail. Web sites can now be repositories of data files, which can be shared over the network with associates worldwide. Instead of having to hire an assistant locally who may not have the best skill set for your business, you can go to the virtual marketplace and identify the most capable of receptionists, bookkeepers, administrative assistants, and the like. The virtual office is here to stay and it eliminates considerable costs to branches, to firms, and to your business.

Trend 10 - Change is a Business Necessity

If your business looks the same today as it did five years ago, you are out of style and out of date. Your clients do not look the same today as they did five years ago and they will not look the same in five more years. The client is constantly changing and your business must do the same. In an interview in Business 2.0, Peter Drucker said that the reason growth companies are innovative, creative, productive, and outpace everyone else is because they ask a question that nobody else asks: "If we weren't doing it this way now would we start doing it this way?"

If the systems and procedures you have in place today are not what you would start doing today, then they need to be adapted or eliminated. Without examining the necessity for change, your client may walk away and you may never even know why.

To help you with this process I created the Finish Well Questions, which you should ask yourself every 90 days. Ask yourself: "What will my life and industry be like in three years?" Look ahead three years and identify the changes that your clients, your industry, and you will make. Secondly, ask: "What can I do today to prepare?" Step into that future. Capture that future. Change your practice. Redesign your business. Use the tools of exponential growth.

The River

A river averages 10 mph over its entire course. In the mountains it flows 15 mph over the rapids and in the lake it flows 0 mph. South of the lake the river widens and eddies -3 mph around the islands in the middle of the river. The river is a metaphor for the stock market.

Your client's portfolio is a rowboat in the river. You, as advisor, are the coxswain, the client the owner and the oarsmen are the money managers. In the lake the oarsmen can row the boat 3 mph. If they continue to outpace the river by 3 mph, is there a difference between the 18 mph in the mountains and the 0 mph in the eddies that the row boat performs? Yes, but is there a difference in the value added by the oarsmen? No, they added the same value at 18 mph as they did at 0 mph.

The reality is they will never row 18 mph in the mountains. Maybe they can row only 12 mph, but they can add greater value in the eddies by rowing 2 mph. They underperform by 3 mph in the mountains and overperform by 5 mph in the eddies.

Like the river, a managed account underperforms in rallies and overperforms in declines. Recall losses have greater negative impact than profits have positive benefit.

The Cowles Commission of 1932

Four Ways to invest safely in the stock market:
* Buy Quality
* Hire Professional Management
* Dollar-Cost Average
* Diversify Assets

50 / 25 / 25 Dollar-cost Averaging

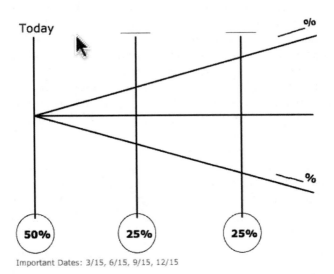

Important Dates: 3/15, 6/15, 9/15, 12/15

There are times when the biggest difficulty you face in business is getting clients to commit their funds to an investment choice. Perhaps they agree with the concept of fee-based assets and even go so far as to say they want to place their money with professional managers, but then the question becomes not so much what to do or how to do it, but more importantly when. When is the best time to make the change and move the assets?

When asked about the best time to invest in the market, Warren Buffet said, "Whenever you have money." Most of the time the market will be higher in the future from a present point in time; 60% to 70% of the time the market will be higher 18 months out than today so Warren Buffet is correct. The best thing you can do whenever you have money is to invest it.

That said, there are two types of money: money at risk in the past and money that was not at risk in the past. If we all had the risk profile and confidence of Warren Buffet to say, "I am setting these funds aside for an unlimited period of time and I will not worry because I will buy good companies and just hold," then we could invest whenever we have the money. Unfortunately, this is not usually the case and we find that many investors are anxious. The stock market is a scary place for them. The funds they invest may never have been in the market before - a rolled over CD or GIC, or funds received from a business sale or real estate sale. These funds may also represent a large portion of a client's total asset base. Therefore, prudence may encourage us to move into the market gradually. Some people like to put their toe in first and test the waters then gradually move in, while others are fine diving in. For "divers" the best thing to do is invest fully whenever they have the money. However, for the ones who want to wade in gradually, we created a model that assists your clients in adding funds to the market on a systematic basis.

I believe there are four important dates for the investment of new funds into the stock market. These dates are March 15th, June 15th, September 15th, and December 15th.

The dates are significant in that they precede the last two weeks of each quarter.

Something significant happens in the market during the last two weeks of a quarter called window dressing. When managers, investment advisors, mutual funds, and institutions liquidate underperforming positions, selling is the order of the day. This practice presents an ideal time for investors to add funds to the market as the institutions are in sell mode.

The dollar-cost averaging model starts with today's date. If the client agrees the investment is a good thing to do, then they put 50% of the money in the market today. Then you determine future investment dates. For instance, if today's date is February 20th, then select March 15th and June 15th as the remaining two date lines. Half the remaining assets, 25% of the total, will be invested into the market on each of these two dates.

Three scenarios can occur in the market after the initial investment of half the assets. Historically, over an 18 month period, the market tends to be up about 70% of the time. The other 30% of the time, the market could be down or flat. If we are bullish and think the market will be up in the future, it would be foolish to hold back part of the funds and wait to invest them later at a higher price. But what if we take a large portion of a client's assets and invest today and then, in 2 months, the market drops significantly? The investment timing seems imprudent and the client might be upset. By using the Dollar-cost Averaging model a disciplined approach to making the investment decision of adding funds to the portfolio is established.

In my practice, when a pool of money accounts for 25% or more of a client's existing assets, the Dollar-cost Averaging model was presented to the client as an alternative to investing all funds at once. If the client agreed, we immediately invested 50% of the assets in the market that day. We then determined the next two investment dates and allocated 25% of the total to be invested on each of those days. The client gave us a market order for those specific dates. My team wrote the order tickets for those dates, but the tickets were not dated for reasons I will explain shortly. My service assistant kept a folder for each of the four important dates: March 15th, June 15th, September 15th and December 15th. When a predetermined date arrived, all order tickets in that folder were executed.

Assume a client has $100,000 to invest, a large portion of their current assets. They agree to invest 50% today, 25% on March 15th, and 25% on June 15th. However, during the period between today and March 15th, the market pulls back and drops 9% below the previous quarter. That means the designated funds can buy at a 9% lower price than originally paid. It is not March 15th yet, but because the market is down 9% from the previous quarter, the folder of order tickets for the next important date are executed now. It is important to note that we never took discretion and contacted clients by phone to explain the opportunity to buy in earlier at a reduced price and to obtain their authorization. If you take discretion in client accounts, you can explain this possible scenario to the client up front.

Along comes March 15th. Since we already invested the funds, we do not do anything until the next quarter's investment date. The market continues to go up. By June 15th, the market is higher. That is alright though because the client understood in advance that 70% of the time they would pay higher prices.

On average, the market may drop 9% inter-year about once every 18 months. If the market drops 18% inter-quarter, take the next two investments, the remaining 50%, and invest them both early. Over the last decade we invested near lows of the cycle by using this model.

When an investor is nervous, the Dollar-cost Averaging model is the best way to get their money into the market. Dollar-cost averaging renders a disciplined approach and the potential to pay significant benefits by investing at or near lows of the period. Even if you do not reap the additional benefit of investing at a lower price, the client still benefits by investing over time without missing the opportunities of a market that on average is up more often than down.

NEXT ACTIONS

The Ten Most Important Things To Do Next

The following pages list the ten actions to take first in implementing the concepts explored in this book. As David Allen says in his book Getting Things Done, determine the next physical action to move you closer to the results you desire.

Ten Most Important Next Actions

1. Identify your Top 20%
- Maintain current business with these households
- Write a personal letter to each
- Conduct Relationship Conversation with each

2. Establish your five model portfolios and select managers.

3. Begin using the Assistant's Script.

4. Bring in all new business under the attraction-based, fee model.

5. Read one book per month about the industry.

6. Join IMCA and become CIMA certified.

7. Begin the Action Plan to fee-based business.

8. Establish a weekly team meeting time and conduct the first meeting.

9. Implement the Creating Exponential Change model with your team.

10. Run DISC Assessments for all team members.

ACKNOWLEDGEMENTS

Those for whom a word of thanks seems insufficient

Many have influenced me through their words or actions. It has always been my hope to draw from those around me and give back more than I receive. Thank you all for your kindness, friendship, and encouragement.

There are so many I need to thank for their encouraging words and support over the years, the following are the ones that stand out from the crowd.

PAMELA, my partner in life and constant inspiration, who encouraged me to write just a few pages every day and edited the drafts.

SHIRLEY ANDERSON, my mentor coach, for her words of wisdom and encouragement.

SUSAN COOPER, my former creative director and webmaster, who edited almost every word I wrote for the industry.

MELANIE DAVIS, my administrative assistant, who has believed in our vision and supported my effort with unfailing loyalty and support.

My TEAM MEMBERS throughout the years, who trusted my vision and gave me the opportunity to pursue my interests.

BILL GOOD, founder of Bill Good Marketing, my first trainer at PaineWebber, who asked me to speak for the first time outside my firm at his Marketing Conference and then encouraged me to create a workshop series for Transitioning to Fees.

HARRY UPTON, my first branch manager, who gave me the opportunity to enter this, the greatest of all industries.

RICHARD HUNTER, my first coach, who held my hand while I made my conversion to fees.

DAVE ECHUS, fellow broker at PaineWebber, who mentored me as a rookie broker into managed money.

SARANO KELLY, my presentation coach, who showed me what it means to be a consummate speaker.

Steve Saenz, founder of Paragon Resources, who introduced me to some of my first corporate clients and has been a dear friend.

John Granzow, who encouraged me to spread my wings and try new things.

Jim Morgan, past chairman of Interstate Johnson Lane, who believed in me despite appearances.

Dan Sullivan, The Strategic Coach, for all the days of focused planning and thought.

My Coaching Clients, who have taught me more about the business since I retired, and finally my workshop clients, who forced me to systematize my message and made this book possible.

BIBLIOGRAPHY

The value of becoming a lifetime learner is unmeasurable

Reading a book is like having a conversation with the author. I have found great inspiration in these conversations and have tried to assimilate the best of their ideas into my life and practice.

Amelio, Gil and Simon, William, *Profit From Experience: The National Simiconductor Story of Transformation Management*, 1996, Van Nostrand Reinhold, New York

Buckingham, Marcus and Coffman, Curt, *First Break All the Rules: What the World's Greatest Managers Do Differently,* 1999, Simon & Schuster, New York

Christensen, Clayton M., *The Innovator's Dilemma: When New Technologies Cause Great Firms to Fail,* 1997, Harvard Business School Press, Boston

Cooper, Robert K. and Sawaf, Ayman, *Executive EQ: Emotional Intellegence in Leadership & Organizations,* 1996, Grosset Putnam, New York

Covey, Stephen, *The 7 Habits of Highly Effective People: Powerful Lessons in Personal Change,* 1990, Fireside, New York

Crawford, Fred and Mathews, Ryan, *The Myth of Excellence: Why Great Companies Never Try to be the Best at Everything,* 2001, Crown, New York

Daley, Kevin and Wolfe, Emmett, *Socratic Selling: How to Ask the Questions that Get the Sale,* 1996, Irwin, Chicago

De Soto, Hernando, *The Mystery of Capital: Why Capitalism Triumphs in the West and Fails Everywhere Else,* 2000, Basic, New York

Drucker, Peter F., *The Essential Drucker,* 2001, Harper Business, New York

Fritz, Robert, *Corporate Tides: The Inescapable Laws of Organizational Structure,* 1996, Herret-Koehler, San Francisco

Fritz, Robert, *The Path of Least Resistance: Learning to Become the Creative Force in Your Own Life,* 1989, Fawcett Columbine, New York

Gerber, Michael E., *The E Myth Contractor: Why Most Contractor's Businesses Don't Work and What to Do About It,* 2002, Harper Business, New York

Gerber, Michael E., *The E Myth: Why Most Small Business Don't Work and What to Do About It,* 1986, Harper Business, New York

Gerber, Michael E., *The E Myth Revisited: Why Most Small Business Don't Work and What to Do About It,* 1995, Harper Business, New York

Gilmore, James H. and Pine, B. Joseph, *Markets of One: Creating Sustomer-Unique Values Through Mass Customization,* 2000, Harvard Business Review, Boston

Goldberg, Marilee C., *The Art of the Question: A Guide to Short-Term Question-Centered Therapy,* 1998, John Wiley, New York

Goleman, Daniel, *Emotional Intellegence,* 1995, Bantam, New York

Grove, Andrew S., *Only the Paranoid Survive: How to Exploit the Crisis Points That Challenge Every Company and Career,* 1996, Currency Books, New York

Grove, Andrew S., *High Output Management,* 1995, Vintage, New York

Hagel, John and Singer, Marc, *Net Worth: Shaping Markets When Customers Make the Rules,* 1999, Harvard Business School Press, Boston

Hamel, Gary, *Leading the Revolution,* 2000, Harvard Business School Press, Boston

Hammer, Michael and Champy, James, *Re-engineering The Corporation: A Manifesto for Business Revolution,* 1993, Harper Business, New York

Harris, Jim, *Blindsided: How to Spot the Next Breakthrough That Will Change Your Business Forever,* 2002, Capstone, Oxford

Harris, Jim, *The Learning Paradox: Gaining Success and Security in a World of Change,* 1998, Macmillan, Toronto

Lencioni, Patrick, *The Five Temptations of a CEO: A Leadership Fable,* 1998, Jossey-Bass, San Francisco

Leonard, Thomas and Laursen, Byron, *The Portable Coach: 28 Surefire Strategies for Business and Personal Success,* 1998, Scribner, New York

Loehr, Jim and Schwartz, Tony, *The Power of Full Engagement: Managing Energy, Not Time, Is the Key to High Performance and Personal Renewal,* 2003, Free Press, New York

Maister, David H., *Managing the Professional Service Firm,* 1993, Freepress, New York

Martin, Chuck, *Net Future: The 7 Cyber Trends that Will Drive Your Business, Create New Wealth, and Define Your Future,* 1999, McGraw-Hill, New York

Maslow, Abraham H., *Maslow on Management,* 1998, John Wiley, New York

McCarthy, Dennis C., *The Loyalty Link: How Loyal Employees Create Loyal Customers,* 1997, John Wiley, New York

Murphy, Kevin J., *Effective Listening: Hearing What People Say and Making it Work for You*, 1987, Bantam Books, Toronto

Novak, Michael, *Business as a Calling: Work and the Examined Life*, 1996, Free Press, New York

O'Neil, John, *Leadership Aikido: 6 Business Practices to Turn Around Your Life*, 1997, Harmony, New York

Peters, Tom, *Thriving on Chaos*, 1987, Borzoi Book, New York

Pine, B. Joseph and Gilmore, James H., *The Experience Economy: Work is Theatre & Every Business a Stage*, 1999, Harvard Business School Press, Boston

Senge, Peter M., *The Fifth Discipline*, 1990, Doubleday, New York

Siegel, Jeremy J., *Stocks for the Long Run: The Definitive Guide to Financial Markets Returns and Long-Term Investment Strategies*, 2002, McGraw-Hill, New York

Stewart, Thomas A., *The Wealth of Knowledge: Intellectual Capital and the Twenty-first Century Organization*, 2001, Currency Book, New York

Swenson, Richard A., *Margin: Restoring Emotional, Physical, Financial, and Time Reserves to Overloaded Lives*, 1992, NavPress, Colorado Springs

Wacker, Watts and Taylor, Jim, *The Visionary's Handbook: Nine Paradoxes That Will Shape the Future of Your Business*, 2000, Harper Business, New York

For more information or to engage Lloyd Williams for speaking, workshops, consulting, or coaching please e-mail info@lloydwilliamsinc.com

The Exponential Business Ltd.

info@lloydwilliamsinc.com

www.LloydWilliamsInc.com

ABOUT LLOYD

Lloyd Williams is an internationally recognized author, executive coach, trainer, and speaker. He has conducted seminars, workshops, and keynote addresses for over a decade. He has conducted workshops for advisors of more than fifty top financial service firms.

Lloyd coaches a select group of executives and entrepreneurs. His coaching guides them toward positive, exponential results in both their personal and professional lives.

Lloyd divides his time between Canada and the United States.

KUTSURO
PRESS

CPSIA information can be obtained at www.ICGtesting.com
Printed in the USA
LVOW07s1440010914

401880LV00019B/918/P